ADVANCE PRAISE

"If you have ever wondered what it might be like to open your own business, read this book. Even if you have no interest in starting a business, the insights in this book are valuable for life in general."

–DR. TASHA EURICH, *New York Times* bestselling author of *Bankable Leadership* and *Insight*

"This book is a must-read for every new start-up. Every entrepreneur needs to learn how to sell and discern good advice from bad. Mike does a great job breaking all of this down through real life examples, many of which I witnessed. *Grind* will be required reading in my classes."

–MICHAEL WILLIAMS, Director of Entrepreneurship Activity & Director of the Business and Entrepreneurship Clinic, University of Wisconsin, Madison

"This book contains the secret recipe for success for entrepreneurs: being all in every day. No one shares their unique energy and enthusiasm like Mike McFall does in *Grind*—an exciting, energizing read for any entrepreneur or entrepreneurs-to-be."

–LILLY STOTLAND, President, Vesco Oil Corporation

"Entrepreneurial wisdom streams from the pages of *Grind*. It reads like a one-on-one conversation with a friend who is sharing the keys to entrepreneurial success—the conversation every aspiring entrepreneur dreams of having!"

–LEE SKANDALARIS, Chief Executive Officer, Quantum Digital Group

"I enjoyed the simplicity of the message. There is no need to make it complicated. Read this book. Stick to the fundamentals and grow your start-up."

–**JEFF DEGRAFF,** PhD, Clinical Professor,
Ross School of Business, University of Michigan

"If more entrepreneurs considered this message it would be great for my business because I would have more late-stage companies to invest in."

–**MICHAEL SOENEN,** Partner, Valor Equity Partners

"Reading this book is like sitting down over a glass of scotch with the author."

–**TREVOR GEORGE,** Founder and
Chief Executive Officer, Blue Wheel Media

"This book is a perfect reflection of its author—both are ruthlessly focused on the personal sacrifice, dedication, and impossibly positive attitude needed to succeed when starting a business."

–**DAVID HEAD,** Managing Director, Alix Partners

"This book reminded me once again what is important in business. I think anyone managing a business should take the time to give it a read."

–**ROB WARK,** Chief Executive Officer,
SAS Global Corporation

"This book dives into the soul of the entrepreneur"

–**SEAN ZECMAN,** President,
National Food Group/Zee Zees

"Having done business with Mike for over two decades, this book rings true to the story and true to the author. It was as much a pleasure reading this book as it has been working with Mike for so many years."

–STEVE MORRIS, President and Chief Operating Officer, Paramount Roasters

"Focus and energy—that is what I feel when I read this book. I think the author would say that is what it takes for a successful start-up. I got it and I love it."

–JOHN JAMES, President, Renaissance Global Logistics and Republican Candidate for US Senate 2018, Michigan

"One hundred percent pure McFall—insightful, humorous, and entertaining. As with all my conversations with Mike, it ended too soon!"

–ED HARDEN, President, Capitol National Bank

"Written with the energy you would expect from an entrepreneur—fast-paced, fun, and direct."

–SAM BEZNOS, Chief Executive Officer, Beztak Companies

MICHAEL J. McFALL

A *No-Bullshit*

APPROACH *TO TAKE*

[**YOUR BUSINESS**]

FROM CONCEPT

TO **CASH FLOW**

AN INC.
ORIGINAL

An Inc. Original
New York, New York
www.anincoriginal.com

Distributed by Greenleaf Book Group

For ordering information or special discounts for bulk purchases, please contact Greenleaf Book Group at PO Box 91869, Austin, TX 78709, 512.891.6100.

Design and composition by Greenleaf Book Group and Brian Phillips
Cover design by Greenleaf Book Group and Brian Phillips
Cover images copyright Jeff Lueders, 2018. Used under license from Shutterstock.com

Publisher's Cataloging-in-Publication data is available.

Print ISBN: 978-1-7325102-6-5

eBook ISBN: 978-1-7325102-7-2

Part of the Tree Neutral® program, which offsets the number of trees consumed in the production and printing of this book by taking proactive steps, such as planting trees in direct proportion to the number of trees used: www.treeneutral.com

Printed in the United States of America on acid-free paper

19 20 21 22 23 24   10 9 8 7 6 5 4 3 2 1

First Edition

To all the owners and operators of BIGGBY COFFEE,
for teaching me everything I know
about business start-ups!

[CONTENTS]

FOREWORD

FIRST, I WOULD LIKE to tell the story of my thirteen-year working relationship with the author, Mike McFall. When we first talked, I worked for Fred Deluca, cofounder of the Subway® franchising organization. At that time, I had just created Franchise Brands, LLC as a vehicle for Fred and his partner to invest in concepts that we could grow through the franchise structure we had developed for Subway restaurants.

My work with the company started when I was a law student and took a summer position to negotiate leases for new Subway locations. At that time, there were 700 Subway sandwich shops. Over the years, my responsibilities in the organization grew to include all aspects of franchise development, I was a member of Fred's Leadership Team, and we had created what we pridefully called a "franchise development machine" through which we added 1,500 locations in more than 100 countries per year.

Now with 27,000 Subway restaurants worldwide, during company strategic planning sessions Fred and I agreed it was time for the company to offer diversified investment opportunities for its stakeholders and for a new challenge for me since the "development machine" was running smoothly. Though the 20 or so years I spent developing the Subway franchise were exhilarating and I would not trade them for anything in the world, I accepted his offer and created an acquisition and investment organization that later became known as Franchise Brands.

Early in the formation of Franchise Brands, Fred expressed interest in investing in a coffee brand. We poled Subway franchise owners regularly about different concepts and coffee was always at the top of the list. Therefore, my team made coffee a priority and we started looking. The company co-owned by author, Mike McFall, was one of the few coffee concepts across the country that were of size and scope that we felt comfortable engaging and was discovered in East Lansing, Michigan, by a member of my team. She gave me the information on the business and then she said, "and you must meet the guys running this thing, they seem to be the real deal." I called and started a conversation that would ultimately lead to thirteen years (and counting) interacting with Mike McFall and Bob Fish, an amazing relationship (the kind of story that fairy tales are written about if there is such a thing as business fairy tales and I believe there are), and my new role as the Chief Development Officer of BIGGBY COFFEE.

A lot has happened over these thirteen years! First, we seriously engaged in deal making three times; each time we came close and in 2015 reached an agreement for Franchise Brands to purchase 50 percent of Bob and Mike's company. However, we tabled the deal at the last minute due to Fred's battle with leukemia; sadly, he passed away just a few months later. Fred was a very smart man who I admired very much. Two of his many amazing qualities were sensing opportunities and understanding people. He loved Bob and Mike and BIGGBY. Over the years he would always ask about them, I would inquire, Mike and I would talk, and talk, and talk. ☺

Fast forward to 2018 when Mike and I had a great exchange as were casually talking and exchanging stories, as we both love to do. I mentioned some improvement he had made in his concept based on a visit from Fred some years ago. He responded that the visits with Fred were incredibly valuable and he always gleaned such powerful insight during those moments. I responded that was what Fred loved about you guys. Mike looked at me with a blank stare. I hit Mike over the head with it, "Mike, you guys did everything Fred suggested and pretty much to the letter." Again, I was met with a blank stare. I continued, "Do you know how many concepts Fred visited? How many entrepreneurs he coached? He made suggestions all the time, every day. People listened, but you guys actually did the stuff he suggested. There was one other important thing he always talked about and that was how you had never been sued by an owner/operator. He loved that because it meant you were good people." Mike laughed as he walked away saying, "What! Are people crazy? Why wouldn't you do exactly what

Fred Deluca suggests?" So few could understand the value of and then execute Fred's suggestions. Mike and Bob always did and still do and always respectfully express appreciation for Fred's guidance.

In my humble opinion, the best teachers are the greatest students—always reading, researching, listening, and trying to get to a deeper understanding. My relationship with Mike has been wonderful, and I have always been impressed with his commitment to learning and getting better at his business. Even though he is a relatively young man, his experience makes him a wily veteran. This book is a fun read, yet it is full of very practical examples and lessons learned over Mike's tenure building the company. I took my new job working within BIGGBY COFFEE because I believe in the company but primarily because I believe in the people, Bob and Mike. They are committed, they are enthusiastic, and they are focused on learning, improving, and therefore growing. And, like Fred, they are committed to creating opportunities for people to grow and I *love* that!

When I finished *Grind*, I sent Mike a note saying every new franchise owner needs to read this. If you read this book and you still want to move forward, then we want you in our system. It goes beyond that though. If you are thinking about opening a new business, I implore you to take the time to read this book, maybe twice. It gives you the flavor and feeling of start-up. It asks you the hard questions. It gives you advice like you would expect from someone who cares deeply for you and your success, from someone who loves you.

Mike told me early on in this project that he wished he could sit down for thirty to sixty minutes with anyone who was starting a new business and share what he'd learned. A new business can be a glorious experience with a wonderful outcome. It can also be an absolute nightmare. Much of what determines which experience you have is the expectation you set going into the new venture. This book will help you set a reasonable expectation for yourself both from a practical standpoint (i.e., "Cut your projected revenue in half, look at the bottom line, if you still want to move forward, I say go for it") and from an emotional standpoint (i.e., "your attitude is the key to your success. Once you start down the negative path it is almost impossible to turn it around"). People just don't talk about mind-set and attitude. They are critical. Set aside a couple of hours and read this book; it will help you with both. I loved it and I am sure you will as well.

One last story before I cut you loose to read this book. Mike and I were standing in the hall the other day as he was awkwardly asking me to write the foreword for his book. He said it felt like when he was in high school and he walked up to the girl he had known since 3rd grade and asked her to the prom. This is truly his blood, sweat, and tears on these pages. The person writing the foreword is like an alter ego. They have to be fully onboard with the words contained within. He originally wanted his partner, Bob, to write this foreword but they agreed they were too close, and it might not come across as genuine, sort of like asking your mother to pen the intro. I was honored and humbled and, of course, I agreed, but I also said, "Boy do I wish Fred were still alive. He would have loved to write the intro for you." As is Mike's way, he looked me dead in the eye and said, "In my opinion, he is." We both teared up for a second and went back to grinding away in our business.

PREFACE

MANY OF THE PEOPLE who I have read on the topic of entrepreneurialism either are so far removed from the start-up phase that they are looking at it through the rose-colored glasses of a nine-figure net worth or are academics who are unaware of how painful the reality of starting a business can be. I am surely not an academic—about as far from it as imaginable—and I am not worth $100 million. I have never had an article written about me in *Fast Company* or *Fortune* or *Entrepreneur* magazine. I don't have an MBA. I am not comfortable with technology and the pace at which social media is warping our context. I am not a "player." I am not ruthless. I am not an absentee parent. I am not a workaholic. I am not fit. My life is comfortable, but I still worry about retirement and schooling my children. I have cried over many failures, and I have celebrated some amazing successes. I don't believe I have all the answers. In fact, as I move forward in life, I learn every day how much I don't know.

However, I am the co-CEO of a successful retail franchise system in the specialty coffee space. I started as a minimum-wage barista in our very first coffee shop and developed the business with my partner. I have spent the last twenty-three years assisting hundreds of people in opening coffee shops—and helped them thrive. Today, BIGGBY COFFEE has 250 stores, and the trajectory of our company is sloping up aggressively. I am no longer in the start-up phase myself, but I walk franchisees—my customers now—through that process every day. My mission with this book is to share what I've learned about the process while my hands are still deep in the mix.

There have been some serious ups and downs in my personal life, but today I am married to a beautiful, dynamic, extreme talent who amazes me daily. I have three children who challenge my humanity more than anything else. My best friends are my two brothers, and I feel connected to my parents in the deepest way. I have been blessed with the greatest business partner, a man full of conviction, character, passion, and ultimately, truth. I have many lifelong friends. I am luckier than anyone I know, and had much luck in the business context of my reality, too. But most of it was commitment and focus to some fundamentals, and that's the part I'll share with you.

Life has been a series of moments that have compounded to form my reality today. It's the same for everyone: reality is both elusive and illusive. Every person perceives the world and their interactions within it from their own context, and every one of those contexts is remarkably dynamic, variable, and subjective.

The only way to understand objective reality is to have authentic and truthful conversations with others. This book is my half of an authentic conversation on starting a business.

My dream would be to chat over coffee with anyone who is opening a business to give them my truth. I hope to share what I have learned over two decades of assisting people in opening their own businesses. Put my experience in your toolbox as you move forward. My most important advice? The key to building a new business to the stage of sustainability—that is, cash flow—is focus. Each time a business owner takes their new business on some tangent, it punches them in the stomach and sets them back. If you can't focus, you can't get to a point of consistent cash flow, and if you can't do that, your business will fail. But if you can focus and stay true to a few principles outlined in this book, you've got a fighting chance to build a sustainable business and, through it, to build wealth.

My advice comes from a place of love, but you might find some of it harsh. That's just tough love. I'd rather you be ready for the reality of a struggle and possible failure than sugarcoat it and ensure failure. Being a successful business owner can go a long way in helping you build a life that you love, but we must first get you to your first day of positive cash flow. Let's get started!

—

Michael J. McFall
Ann Arbor, Michigan, 2018

Chapter 1

DUE DILIGENCE

WELCOME TO THE WORLD of entrepreneurship. It's a unique club. There are no barriers to entry—no barriers based on historical paradigms, age, religious preference, sexual orientation, race, height, or gender. All that matters is whether you can figure out how to sell an enormous amount of stuff in the marketplace with an appropriate gross margin. Sounds easy, but what most people don't realize is that the biggest barrier to success is themselves.

For as long as you can remember, you've obsessed about new business ideas and aching needs in the marketplace. Some ideas were good, but let's be honest, most of them were a little off the mark. That T-shirt business in high school? European vacation–inspired kebab shops near college campuses? Mid-January Michigan–inspired full-service gas stations? The mechanism that makes putting a baby seat in a car simple? An app that tracks city bus progress? And on and on.

Now that you've reached this point, you can't ignore this entrepreneurial itch or you'll go nuts—or worse, look back on your life with regret. No more being envious of the neighbor who owns seven Subway sandwich locations and seems to have gobs of money and all the free time in the world, always gardening and spending time with the kids. You finally have your idea. No more scribbling on bar napkins and backs of envelopes. No more energized "what if" conversations only to wake up the next day and go back to your monotonous routine. Now you believe in yourself and your idea with every cell in your body. It's time to execute! Let's roll!

New business owners are among the most optimistic people on the planet. That's why I love working with them. But that optimism serves a more evolutionary purpose: in the face of all the inevitable and unexpected pitfalls, especially during the start-up phase, an obnoxiously positive attitude is a necessary survival tool. But to survive what?

Everyone has a degree of entrepreneurial spirit, yet only 16 percent of Americans own their own business.[1] Why? Because you have to be the right kind of crazy and believe in yourself completely to even try, first. Second, the failure rate of new enterprises is astronomical. According to *The One Minute Entrepreneur* by Kenneth Blanchard, Don Hutson, and Ethan Willis (with

---

1   "90% of American workers don't own their own business, Rick Santorum says," Politifact.com, accessed December 13, 2018, https://www.politifact.com/truth-o-meter/statements/2015/apr/13/rick-santorum/90-american-workers-dont-own-their-own-business-ri/.

figures updated from the Bureau of Labor Statistics), "Within any given year, close to 1 million people start a small business in the United States. Sadly, at least 20 percent of those businesses fail within the first year. 64.3 percent of them will be out of business within 10 years."[2,3] More remarkably, just 0.04 percent will reach $100,000,000 in annual sales;[4] out of approximately 550,000 start-ups with employees, only between 125 and 250 companies will reach that level.[5] Odds for success are low.

As my good friend Dr. Green likes to say, "It isn't all sushi and puppy parties." You accept it, you understand the statistics, you know the risks, and, even with all of the naysayers, you are ready to make the leap.

What next? This book is an invitation to come and sit in my backyard at my picnic table. You are drunk with enthusiasm; you accept my invitation and fly to Ann Arbor, Michigan, for lunch. The barbecue is on the grill, and my dog is chasing bugs around the yard while snacking on poop. My beautiful

2   Kenneth Blanchard, Don Hutson, and Ethan Willis, *The One Minute Entrepreneur* (New York: Doubleday, 2008).

3   "Business Employment Dynamics: Entrepreneurship and the U.S. Economy," Bureau of Labor Statistics, accessed December 5, 2018, https://www.bls.gov/bdm/entrepreneurship/bdm_chart3.htm.

4   Bill Carmody, "Only 0.04 Percent of Companies Reach $100 Million in Annual Revenue. Here's the 1 Thing Driving YapStone's Explosive Growth," Inc.com, December 24, 2015, https://www.inc.com/bill-carmody/only-0-04-reach-100-million-in-annual-revenue-here-s-the-one-thing-driving-yapst.html.

5   Paul Kedrosky, "The Constant: Companies that Matter," Kauffman Foundation, May 10, 2013, https://www.kauffman.org/what-we-do/research/2013/05/the-constant-companies-that-matter.

wife insists on giving you a tour of the house before she brings her famous cucumber salad as a starter.

It is driving you crazy. You are dying to dive into it, so let's get down to business. I reach over, grab a mirror. I ask if you are ready to engage in the most important conversation in your professional life. I ask if you are ready to start the only process that matters to the success of your new business. "Yes, yes, of course," you say. We are going to start the due diligence process—due diligence on you. I hold the mirror up in front of you.

You are the number one ingredient, the most powerful factor in whether your new business will succeed or fail. Your mind-set, your enthusiasm, your attitude, and your commitment are the most powerful influences on the success of your new enterprise by a factor of ten. The leading indicator in your business is you, your self-awareness, your attitude.

I watch people do hundreds of hours of due diligence. They research everything there is to research, including the following:

- Capital structure: What is the precise level of leverage that is appropriate?
- Real estate data: What is the right dirt and why?
- SWOT analysis to provide insight into the competitive landscape
- Financial analysis with pro forma data to provide complex ratios on cash flow
- Marketplace metrics to show size of market, with a .01 percent capture rate equating to success

- Complex demographics to explain consumer buying power and predict the size of the market
- Consumer behavior trends with in-depth analysis of millennial behavior: How best to capture this powerful force in a particular market?
- Personality profiles on team members: How are they going to contribute?
- Exit strategies, valuation methods, clawback provisions, and cap tables in the event it all doesn't work

All these types of data are good to think about, and this kind of due diligence is certainly important. Yet almost all of the lists I see are missing the most crucial bullet point: YOU!

I can hear the collective sigh from academics out there. But let me assure you, a perfect understanding of the marketplace will not make your business successful. Before you even start examining unintended costs, market forces, and competition, you must have a clear, comprehensive understanding of yourself.

The franchise business pretty much models a controlled study to prove this point. McDonald's, like any other well-organized franchise, offers the same system and product to all of their franchisees. Some people take those tools and make them work, and they are wildly successful. Others use those same tools and fail. What's the difference? I think it's obvious, but what is scary is how few people will acknowledge this fact. There have been hundreds and hundreds of different coffee shop concepts started in America over the past twenty-five years. How many have gotten to over $100 million in revenue? Fewer than ten. What is the difference? At the sake of sounding arrogant, the difference is my partner and me versus everyone else.

We have spent more than twenty years in the trenches. We have both mopped the floors and cleaned the toilets, hundreds of times. We both have had social engagements squashed by last-minute call-ins, hundreds of times. We both have had customer interactions that teetered on psychotherapy, hundreds of times. Most importantly, we both knew the other had our back. We knew the other was a gift and must be respected. We both knew that it could all go away in a split second, and we still feel that way today. In the end, this is our start-up, our mission; this is who we are and what we do. There is nothing else.

We have battle scars. There is a little limp when we first get out of a chair. We carry a trace of dried blood under our fingernails. My partner's right shoe is untied because he won't take the time to bend over and make a bow. But even today, twenty-plus years later, the twinkle is still in our eyes. Unbridled enthusiasm got us to where we are, and if you ask either one of us, we will tell you we are just getting started.

The greatest things in life are generally the hardest things. Starting a business can be remarkably rewarding, but it can also be extremely difficult. Let's see if you are up for the challenge. Accomplishing the proper due diligence on yourself requires strict attention to a few crucial traits you must be aware of and bring with you—or not—every day to your start-up. If you don't have these positive qualities in spades, or they're not your strong suits, then work on them; build them up every single day. The same holds true for getting rid of the negative ones. It takes time and focus, but this stuff is critical.

This first chapter is devoted to helping you do due diligence on yourself. It's essential to take the time to think about you, because how you think and what you feel is the only thing that matters when it comes to whether your business will die in the start-up phase or make it to its first dollar in cash flow. It might seem obvious at first, but I see new business owners over and over who can't get out of their own way, and it usually doesn't end well. That's because they weren't thinking about these ten crucial steps in doing due diligence on themselves:

- Grow in self-awareness.
- Make friends with the boogieman.
- Be patient with the results but aggressive in execution!
- Be humble, curious, and ready to learn.
- Muster massive doses of energy and enthusiasm.
- Model dependability and dedication.
- Tap into the secret of focus.
- Be gentle with your internal control freak.
- Gut-check your ego.
- Name the end game.
- The powerful stuff is simple.

GROW IN SELF-AWARENESS

If the single most important factor of a start-up's success is you, then the single most important *quality* that you must have is self-awareness.

At first glance, there might not seem to be much of a difference here, but it is one of my most powerful points. We could simply rephrase the whole thing to say: you actually aren't the most important ingredient to the success of your business, but your self-awareness is.

Nobody is perfect. Not a single one of us has all the traits and qualities that make up the perfect founder who can launch a new business and make it profitable. On any given day, you may be fired up to make sales calls and talk to anyone you meet about your fabulous new product. Another day, you may not want to leave your office or pick up the phone ever again.

We are all human. We have our good days and bad days, and on each you're going to be strong in some areas and weaker in others. So it goes. The key is to understand this cycle and develop a strategy to take care of your business by working hard to understand what you need around you to offset and counterbalance . . . you!

It's important to take honest stock of yourself. I know it sounds cheesy and cliché, but you really do need to take a look in the mirror. What are your strengths, and how do you leverage them? What are your flaws (limitations?), and how do you compensate for them?

What are the traits I recommend you evaluate before you get started? There are many, but what I want to give you is a look into the ones I feel are most important—the fundamentals. These are the quirks, the things that most people don't look at before getting started with their new business, but to me this is the gold. This is the stuff that nobody else is thinking about but the stuff that is most important and will make all the difference.

MAKE FRIENDS WITH THE BOOGIEMAN

Your start-up will punch you in the gut nearly every single day. That's a given. The only uncertainty is where that punch will come from. I like to call it the boogieman behind the tree. When you're walking along the path, minding your own business (literally), you never know when the next boogieman is going to jump out and take a swipe at you. It won't jump out at the same time every day, or from the same angle, but the next one is always coming.

Being aware that the boogieman exists is healthy. But if you let the boogieman affect you as you're running your business—if you're paranoid and glancing behind every tree—you're in trouble.

Being out on your own is hard. Building a start-up is one of the most difficult things you can do. I haven't met a single business owner who has said, "Gee, that was much easier than I thought it would be." But if you let all that difficulty get to you, if you let it shake your confidence and deplete your energy and enthusiasm, it will determine how you present yourself to the world, and your chance of success in the business will be greatly diminished.

Let me share a scary tale about when I got punched (and

kicked, and punched again) by the biggest, most powerful boogieman I have encountered: the bank.

Back in 2003, only eight years into our business, my partners and I purchased and converted a six-store chain of coffee shops called Sufficient Grounds into BIGGBY. We operated it for about a year, and business was mediocre at first but improving. We had borrowed a significant sum to purchase and convert the stores. We were never late on our loan payments, and I was sending regular financial statements to the banker. One day, I got a call from said banker, who invited himself to my office with his boss. A call out of the blue from your banker, who says he's bringing his boss over to chat? Red blinking lights started going off like fireworks in my head. Here comes the boogieman.

The two bankers arrived and proceeded to tell me that our business was outside some covenants of the loan agreement and they were putting us in default. Now, I'm going to let you in on a little secret: I had no idea what being in default meant. Ignorance can be bliss, but had I known what I was in for, I would have been smart to simply give up. **Critical point:** Any successful business owner will have a story like this, in which they say, "If I had known at that moment what I was up against, I would surely not have kept going." But in my experience, the successful ones never stop, never give up. Please understand I am not advocating ignorance. I am suggesting you will find yourself in situations where your naiveté will land you in difficulty, and nobody is experienced enough to avoid this spot. What I am advocating is those who succeed are the ones who never threw in the towel, those who never gave up, those willing to succeed or die trying. Remember Ray Kroc was in his fifties when he started McDonald's.

After settling into a table with their BIGGBY lattes (on the house), the bankers proceeded to explain that through a random selection of accounts, they had done a review of our file, and quite simply our free cash flow wasn't appropriate to our debt service. They politely reminded me that I had signed a contract that said I'd keep this ratio within a set range. We were outside that range, and we were being put into default.

I was more than a bit naïve about how much power bankers wield. I was about to find out what a loan default actually meant and felt like.

The bank assigned to us what is called a "workout specialist." This person's job is to liquidate the company and get as much money back as possible. Basically, their job is to be as big a jerk as possible, and from my experience, they are quite good at it. I mean, these folks come from the same delightful talent pool as bouncers and prison guards.

The workout specialist raised our interest rate from 7 to 11.5 percent, nearly doubling our monthly payment. They took every dime of cash from the business and cleaned out our personal bank accounts. They set up a separate account to capture all of our revenue from all entities. In short, they were perfectly comfortable putting us out of business because we didn't have a penny anywhere to spare. Every penny that wasn't mission critical to the business went to pay down debt.

While all this was going on, we still had other stores and employees to manage and owner-operators to support. Every week from Sunday to Wednesday, I drove two hours each way to manage one business in Toledo to try and placate the bank that was threatening to take everything we had. The remaining part of the week I worked at the home office to help manage and grow the rest of our business. It was incredibly stressful. I still had to meet with prospective buyers, put on my sales hat, and champion the company. It took a lot of energy to force a smile with a friend, much less a stranger. But smile I did; I even laughed. In front of customers, I remained BIGGBY's biggest cheerleader, even though I knew it was distinctly possible that everything could evaporate. If I couldn't compartmentalize the fierce attack the boogieman was raining down on me, it would all be over. Eight years of my life flushed.

In the face of my company's impending implosion, if we had flinched even the slightest, if I had failed to bring my usual energy and enthusiasm to my staff meetings or to my conversations with potential franchisees or customers, they surely would have noticed. Before long, the boogieman would've dealt his death blow.

How much positive energy and enthusiasm will you bring to work on your darkest days? The days the boogieman has kicked you in the groin, kneed you in the nose, and has you in a headlock, giving you a noogie. Will you be your business's biggest cheerleader at this moment? How will you answer questions about how your business is doing? The boogieman is powerful, and he defeats most people; are you ready to poke the boogieman in the eye, kick him in the groin, and then laugh in his face with a huge smile on your face? You had better be, because he is coming after you, I promise.

BE PATIENT WITH THE RESULTS BUT AGGRESSIVE IN EXECUTION!

If I have learned one thing in my career, it's that nothing happens as quickly as I would like. Patience is one of the fundamental keys to success in any start-up. It is the rare endeavor that ramps up quickly, and if your start-up does, you should consider yourself lucky: you won the lottery. If it does, you can scoff at the premise of my book, and I will sincerely congratulate you for a job well done. Most of us, though, must be patient. Patience isn't about being OK with time passing; patience isn't about accepting any eventuality. Patience is making sure you are sticking to your knitting, knowing it is going to work in the end—doing the right things day in and day out, knowing the results will show up.

Over the years, I have seen countless people grow impatient and start cutting corners because the proven methods aren't producing quickly. In the end, the shortcuts impede the performance of the business, and whatever momentum was building slows and eventually goes away. In my business, we advocate the same model to everyone. One of the saddest things I see is an operator who is losing faith and starts to cut corners when they were only a few feet, moments, customers away from it all working.

Impatience breeds disappointment. If you are disappointed in your business, you will be lacking one of the primary fundamentals: enthusiasm. Once you are headed down this dark path of disappointment, it is hard to turn back. It is a pretty exceptional person who can turn it around once they are in the swamp of disappointment.

Impatience stems from going into the business with unrealistic expectations. It is something I work on constantly in my business. If you think you should be cash flowing and managing the business from your back patio with cocktail in hand by month nine, you are headed for a train wreck of disappointment. It can happen, it has happened, but it isn't going to happen to you. You are in for a long, slow struggle. Are you going to be patient? Are you going to nurture the business? Are you going to show up and execute daily, perfectly, and give the business the time it needs to mature and develop revenue?

Typically, impatience is bred by a lack of cash. The business isn't generating enough sales. You are negative cash flowing, and therefore you decide to cut back on some things to save money to preserve your cash and fight another day. This is logical and almost a visceral reaction at the moment. The problem is, it doesn't work. Once you start going down this path, it becomes a never-ending process of small cuts to save the business. Once this mentality has set in, it is the first step in the demise of the business. You have to stay patient and figure out how to get the money while executing perfectly and aggressively. Easy to say, difficult to do.

Some examples might be helpful. One of the first and easiest things to cut in any budget is advertising. Proving that an advertising campaign is working is nearly impossible. The dollars are usually pretty big and are easy to cut. But if you stop promoting your business and expect your revenue to grow, you are in a delusional state. The mistake is so obvious. Second is to start cutting labor, just a few well-timed hours here and there at the beginning, but three months later you are running with a skeleton crew. If you are committed to providing human interaction in your business at launch but the person answering the phone is expensive, you go with an automated system. In my business, you start to run with one barista on the floor in the evening. It makes sense; the evening is slow. A few months later it makes sense to cut it to one barista in the afternoon on certain days. But the result of all these labor cuts is that the customer experience suffers and you end up with fewer customers.

Probably my most extreme example of impatience and the need to save money to survive was an owner-operator who rationed whipped cream at a store. He allowed the store five bottles of whipped cream to start the day. When it was gone it was gone; nobody else would get whipped cream. The list goes on.

There is only one decision to be made—get more money, keep operating at the highest level and be patient, or shut down and lick your wounds. Getting more money is difficult, almost impossible, but so it goes. Figure it out or sail away on the ship of lost hopes and dreams.

BE HUMBLE, CURIOUS, AND READY TO LEARN

Arrogance and ignorance are the ingredients in the worst-tasting bowl of slop ever produced. Arrogance is ignorance. Anyone who believes they have the answers is destined for the proverbial train wreck. By definition, if you have never opened a business before, you should consider yourself ignorant on the topic. Blend in arrogance, which is going to get in the way of you believing in your need to learn, and you have a recipe for disaster or a bowl of horrible-tasting slop.

The great proprietors, the ones I have watched and read about who grow start-ups into successful enterprises, are the ones who are confident in their ability—their ability to learn and adapt. One of their biggest assets is that they know they have a ton to learn in their new enterprise. They know how much they don't know about making it successful. They are committed to learning and growing both themselves and their business.

Being the owner of a franchise company, I get to see this dynamic unfold firsthand. The barrier to entry is fairly steep, and to make the necessary capital investment, you most likely were accomplished in some other area of life and/or business. Based on the successes of your previous life, you may feel cocksure and ready to execute. Naturally and logically, you are confident. But execute what? If you are investing in a franchise, are you ready to learn and execute the franchise model flawlessly? First, in our business you must understand that you don't know much about building a successful coffee shop. Second, you must be willing to learn everything about the system and wake up every day ready to execute said system—every detail. If you execute every detail that you learn, my prediction is you will do well in the business. If you enter our world thinking you know "business," if you are confident in your ability to manage and grow a business, and if all of our processes and systems seem a tedious burden, my prediction is you will struggle. How hard can it be to run a coffee shop anyway?

My advice, whenever I have the opportunity to give it to a new operator entering our world, is to take the first two years of operation and treat it like you are going back and getting a master's degree in the retail gourmet coffee business. Therefore, a big part of your initial investment in the business is the educational component of the first two years. At the end of two years, much of what we recommend and advocate—the system—will make sense to you, I promise. At the end of two years, I am ready to sit down and get your feedback and try to improve what we are doing. At the end of two years, you are ready to go and start actually building your business on top of the foundation of what you have learned. The launching point of your business is not the day you open; it is 730 days into the business.

If you are starting a business from scratch, not entering a franchise, this process is longer. I think it is at least double. In our business it took five to seven years. We hadn't figured out the model, and we didn't understand the nuances of the business that would allow us to make any real money for a very long time. There was so much to learn, so much to get organized. It is a long, slow, difficult process.

Gut check: Are you prepared to commit years of your life to the educational process, learning the business in order to prepare yourself to increase the value of your asset after this initial period? Are you humble enough to admit you don't know this business and you have a ton to learn? If so, I think you are in the right frame of mind to be successful in your new start-up enterprise. However, if you scoff at the thought of this extended period of education and are thinking instead, *I am going to get my original investment back in two years*, I think you need to consider that arrogance is likely to get in the way of your success.

Also, I think you need to consider that your expectations of yourself and your new business are way too high.

This little tidbit of wisdom isn't new, of course. The roots go all the way back to Socrates, who wrote: "I know that I am intelligent, because I know that I know nothing." And more magazine articles, speeches, and advice books have been devoted to this idea that it's almost a cliché.

But speaking of clichés, if you're into putting motivational quotes up on your fridge or bedroom mirror or office desk, add this one: "It takes a confident person to admit they don't know everything." Humility is one of the key ingredients to success in your start-up. If you admit that you know little about the business and commit yourself to learning every nuance, then you are starting from a healthy place, and your chances of success go up dramatically.

Example: We worked with a gentleman who came from a family business that had been wildly successful over multiple generations. His brother was managing the business, and our guy wanted to prove he was worthy and capable at building a successful business. In one of our first meetings, he committed to becoming our biggest BIGGBY COFFEE operator within five years. He had huge amounts of capital behind him and enthusiasm to burn. Today, red flags would be popping off everywhere, but back then, I was super excited to get this guy going. He chose a high-profile market, and before we knew it he had signed a lease and was charging forward. He didn't accept our model. He signed a lease that was double the cost of our highest limits. He brought on a full-time, high-dollar manager from day one. He put money into his space that we advised against.

All the while we were trying to coach him away from these expenditures. It wasn't our system; it wasn't what had worked for us to date. The first store opened to a resounding thud. He was selling very little coffee. This isn't an uncommon result in new markets with little brand recognition.

We advised him to hunker down, get rid of the highly paid manager, put an apron on, and work in the store. He needed to figure out how to sell a ton of coffee from that location for himself. If he didn't figure out how to sell cups of coffee, he had no future. This is the learning curve. He ignored us and signed a second lease that was more expensive than the first. His thinking was that more brand recognition in the market would help his first store. Only a couple of months after opening store number one, he left it in the hands of his manager, who was also arrogant and, not surprisingly, ignored most of what we were advocating. The owner then went on to store number two, which also opened with a resounding thud. Now he had double the trouble. It lasted another six months, and then he realized he needed to make a change. He fired the manager and started running both stores. One year later he sold them both at a huge loss and walked away, giving us the middle finger as if it had been our fault.

The success of his family business, which was in retail, had produced unfounded arrogance. He thought he knew business, he thought he knew retail, and he was going to show us how to get it done, for real!

MUSTER MASSIVE DOSES OF ENERGY AND ENTHUSIASM

Your personal energy and enthusiasm are the fuel needed for your start-up. You are the primary energy source for your business. The business will require everything from you, and it will drain your tank empty most days. You have to wake up tomorrow and provide your business with the fuel it needs. And you have to do it again the next day, and then every day after that until the cash is flowing—whether that's in 90 days or 914.

Would your best friend describe you as one of the most energetic and enthusiastic people they know? If not, I would consider this a significant hurdle you face. Your business will be a mirror image of you. If you lack energy and enthusiasm, so will your business, and the business will struggle to get traction.

So, the obvious question that begs is, can you be successful in business as an introvert? Yes, of course, but you have to be self-aware enough to recognize how it is going to get in your way. My partner is a classic introvert, the guy at a party leaning up against the wall hoping somebody will come up to him and talk. He is not naturally outgoing or gregarious. He knows the situations in our business when he needs to put his costume on and act the part. He knows when the superhero cape gets strapped on, and he ups the animation. I equate this to being an actor. Do you have to be an extrovert to play an extrovert on stage? Nope. In business you simply need to figure out when you need to play the extrovert and then figure out how to do it.

Can you be told six reasons why your business sucks today, put your ego in your pocket, and continue to act enthusiastically while bringing overwhelming positive energy and enthusiasm to the business with a firm belief in what you are doing and that it is going to work? Put in the simplest terms possible, will you be able to ignore all the negativity, all the doubters, and fake it until you have made it? What? This can't be right. Fake it? Yep, there is no better way to say it. In business, people will avoid a loser. They will avoid the negative. You need people to believe in you; you need people to be willing to come along for the ride. You will get kicked in the baby maker every day, and nobody can know. You have to be the beacon—the North Star—and everyone will follow you. Even when you are having a horrible day, you must bring the positive energy; you have to find it within yourself, and if you are miserable, you have to fake it. You must make people believe, even if at times you don't.

If you walk into most new businesses and ask how they are doing, the typical reply will be "It's been a little slow" or "We are doing OK; we are hanging in there." The customer leaves with the feeling that business isn't so good, and it is a question mark whether it will make it. First, people want to be with a winner, not a loser. If your lack of enthusiasm toward the business shines through, you are going to be in trouble. Second, and most important, your people will feed off of you. They are your primary tool to communicate with your customers. They will believe if you believe; they will be negative if you are negative. If you expect them to be positive and energetic about the business when you aren't, this is irrational. Your positive energy and your enthusiasm for the business are mission critical.

Example: My business partner offers one of the great examples of this mentality. At the beginning of our first store, the business was generating almost zero revenue. People would pull into the empty parking lot and walk into the store, and it was like a ghost town—not a great feeling for the customer. My partner would have the steam wand going full tilt at the espresso machine. He would hit the extraction button and be wiping the counter vigorously. As the customer walked to the counter, he would exclaim, "Phew, we just got through a rush! What can I get for you?" He would say this before the customer could even really think about the fact that it was slow. Everyone would ask, "How is business?" His answer: "Way better than we expected. It has been amazing!" Neither of which are lies; we had the expectation of pending bankruptcy, and it has been amazing, amazingly horrible. In this scenario, the customer leaves with the feeling that the business is really working and going to be successful. They are compelled to come back.

MODEL DEPENDABILITY AND DEDICATION

Will you walk through a brick wall to get your business to the finish line where cash flows positive? Are you willing to accept that everything is your fault when it doesn't work and give all the credit to somebody else when it does? Will you always be there on time, and be prepared? Even when nobody is looking? If not, please don't get started.

In your new business, if you're not on time, nobody cares. If you're not prepared for every meeting, the world keeps on moving along undisturbed; nobody even notices. The only source of accountability you have is the performance of your business. If your business isn't performing, it is simply a reflection of you. If you're not prepared every day, your people will notice, and they will reflect you.

Which brings me to vacation and sick days. They become few and far between, *very* few and far between. You know what I'm going to say. That's right. In a start-up, there are no days off. Maybe you head "up north" every year for a week in August, or travel to see family over the holidays. Sorry. The family traditions have to be put on hold. There will be no vacations or holiday breaks until you get that cash to flow, and flow for a while.

If your plan is to be all in for the first six months or year, and then hire someone and count on your experience and MBA to manage the business, you are setting yourself up for failure. You must be the number one example, the most committed teammate, for a very long time. During start-up you cannot hire the number one example. In my twenty years I have never seen it work.

"Show, don't tell" is the only way it can work in a start-up. Your customers, your vendors, your employees—your significant other, even—must see and feel your dedication. That means you must show up every day, put your helmet on and mouthpiece in, grab the controls, lock in, and go for it. You, and only you, set the tone.

If that's not your level of commitment to this business, keep your money in the proverbial pocket. There isn't a single person who is involved with our company who doesn't know and feel that my business partner and I will do whatever it takes, whenever it's needed, in order to make the business grow and thrive.

I was fortunate to play golf in an event this summer with a young up-and-coming golfer. He is an extreme talent. He is fortunate to be mentored by one of the great athletes of all time, Michael Jordan. He told me that Michael told him, "You will never be pleasantly surprised with an outcome. If you are *hoping* to perform at the highest level, you won't." You must know that you will perform at the highest level. The only way to do that is to be perfectly dedicated to working and preparing. Working hard is what will allow you to believe in you. There are no pleasant surprises. Your effort level will directly correlate to your belief, and your belief is the only thing that matters to your success. Are you willing to try harder at your new business than you have ever tried at anything in your life? Are you willing to be the most dedicated and dependable person in your start-up for seven to ten years? If not, stay home.

As for illnesses, who are you going to call if you get sick? Even if you have a partner, they can't cover your work while staying on top of theirs. Get your flu shot, take vitamin C, work out, and, if you're like me, always have some gauze handy.

Example: One Monday morning when I was managing our second store, I showed up with a huge cut on my chin. I love to play hockey, and the night before I'd had a run-in with the end of a hockey stick in a men's league game. I didn't go to the ER, as it was well after midnight and I knew I'd probably be there until dawn, and I had to be at the store at five fifteen a.m. Instead, I patched it up with a bunch of gauze and a few butterfly bandages and went to bed. I thought everything was fine until the next morning, when I went to ring up one of my first customers and he said, "Dude, you gotta fix that." My makeshift field dressing hadn't held, and I had blood dripping down my neck. Picture a barista version of Dan Aykroyd's legendary send-up of Julia Child on *Saturday Night Live.*

I realized that going to work that morning wasn't sanitary and was off-putting to the customer. I didn't have any options. Had I gotten stuck at the emergency room waiting to get stitched up, no one would have been there to open the store. As a fledgling new business, we didn't have the luxury of missing out on a Monday morning's revenue. Every penny mattered.

TAP INTO THE SECRET OF FOCUS

On occasions when I have the opportunity to speak in front of student groups, they ask how we have been able to get BIGGBY to the stage and size it is today, and what has made us successful. I always have a one-word answer: focus. We have been focused on one thing, and one thing only, for twenty years. We sell cups of coffee. We sell cups of coffee to people as a regular part of their daily lives. We don't have soups, salads, or sandwiches. We don't have beer and wine. We didn't roll in an elaborate gelato offering. This is all a mess, and they get in the way of selling one more cup of coffee today. We do coffee really, really well! Period.

At times, there has been pressure on my partner and me to complicate the menu. We have refused. Could we have had a full-on lunch menu? Could we have said, "Let's add ice cream"? In the evenings, when the coffee business is slow, could we have gone ahead and added wine and beer? Of course. And we thought about all of those things. But it always kept coming back to the question: What are we? Are we a coffee shop that has a happy hour? If we throw in food, does that make us a bistro? Entrepreneurs often lack focus, especially at the beginning when they aren't cash flowing. They are always searching for an answer. The answer is in the fundamentals of the original business you started. Focus on your core business/product, make it amazing, make it perfect. If the market doesn't buy it, move on, shutter it, and live to fight another day. Complexity in a start-up is a web that tangles you up and keeps you from focusing on and doing what is most important—selling a ton of your core products. If it doesn't relate to selling a ton of your core product, don't do it.

If your business isn't working, don't try to bolt on more stuff and add complexity to solve it. Go the other way: simplify and focus on what you do best.

Example: I have a good friend who invested in his buddy's pizza restaurant. The guy had managed a long-established pizza joint in town, and my friend gave him $100K to go open his own place. Then another $50K. Then $100K more.

By the time he called me, my friend had invested $350,000 in his buddy's failing pizza restaurant. My friend had a solution and called me giddy with excitement; they wanted to open a BIGGBY inside of his pizza place. He couldn't wait to bring me the deal. He had it all figured out.

I was a bucket of cold water. After a long pause I replied, "This is a horrible idea. You are a smart guy; we both know it. You are making this thing way too complicated." His buddy hadn't even figured out how to sell pizzas yet, and he wanted to add a coffee shop? The coffee shop would simply be a distraction; it wasn't going to help them sell more pizzas, and the complexity of the operation by adding coffee would make his buddy a worse operator in the pizza business.

It wasn't going to work. You can't add complexity to save a business in the start-up phase. Don't bolt on more stuff—you'll just make it sink faster and exhaust yourself while doing it. Put every ounce of energy into selling one more pizza tomorrow. If you can't figure out how to sell one more pizza tomorrow, shut down the business, lick your wounds, and move on.

BE GENTLE WITH YOUR INTERNAL CONTROL FREAK

Perfectionism is a double-edged sword. There's a fine line in the start-up phase between using the pursuit of perfection to make your business the best and letting perfection get in the way of your main goal, which is to figure out how to sell your product and turn on the spigot of cash.

Often, I see people struggle by focusing on getting things perfect before they have even gotten started. I find it is usually a symptom of an even bigger problem: they don't like sales (much more on this in chapter 2). You need to blow through the details; you need to get things well enough under control so you can sell product and deliver. Free yourself so you can spend your time figuring out how to generate revenue.

In a start-up, the meter is always running. I'm not saying skip the due diligence and planning, but if you wait until everything is exactly how you envisioned it, you'll get bogged down in silly details and miss many opportunities to sell your product. You'll be riddled with anxiety over the terms of the agreement on the office coffee program, or the office furniture being the wrong color, or the shade of the secondary blue on your logo being too light and bleeding away. All this stuff is distracting from what is important, and I watch almost everybody do it to one degree or another. Typically, it centers on your area of expertise prior to your start-up. If you were in graphic design and the visual arts, the colors of your logo are going to be earth-shatteringly important to you. If you were a computer programmer, you are going to obsess over the technology.

Perfect is the enemy of good enough! In nearly every aspect of the business, you simply have to be good enough. The one exception is in your customer interaction. It must be perfect.

Take leases, for example. Any smart businessperson who has been around the block can tell you the thirty things to look out for in a lease. If you listen to them, you will struggle to get the deal done and your business opportunity will stall. With a start-up, a landlord is going to be much more conservative; they need to be covered. Down the road, once you are established, you can get twenty-eight out of thirty things covered. For now, just get it done. Don't worry about every clause in a lease; get the fundamentals square (like price, term, and the guarantee) and move on to more important things. Spend an afternoon and $900 getting the big things right, not three weeks and $5,000 dealing with every little nuance your attorney uncovers.

Be wary of obsessing about liability. I've seen too many people get mired in details, worrying about limiting their exposure one clause at a time. This is precious time taken away from maximizing your upside. When you're focusing on the upside, the revenue, you're focusing on the customer. And the business will grow. When you are obsessing about covering your downside, you are acting from a base of fear, and fear is a huge impediment to progress.

It's deadly to let your mind wrap around what could happen if something goes wrong. There are risks to starting a business that are unavoidable, and yes, they can leave you exposed. You have to figure out a way to get to the point where you can say, "Enough—I'm going to focus on the customer, and I am going to start generating revenue" and let the chips fall where they may. If you can't get to this point, if you are obsessing over the details, I predict doom.

The key is to start getting the revenue in the door. One of the best examples in my world was that big, bad Ohio bank boogieman. Had I understood what covenants in a loan were—or what a default looks and feels like—I may not have signed the agreement that financed our first acquisition, the one that propelled us to a new level of legitimacy. We purchased six stores in a different state. That move helped us sign another twenty or thirty operators in our home state; it took us to the next level. Had I gotten bogged down in the legalities of the bank debt agreement, my growth would have been an entirely different animal, maybe a turtle as opposed to a hare.

All lawyers out there, please try to start breathing again. It will all be OK. With this mind-set we will generate enough revenue to pay you to get us out of the jams in which we will eventually find ourselves. (Please allow me to take a sidebar: I love lawyers. Anybody who makes lawyer jokes or gets angry about how lawyers work or bill has never been in a serious bind with a good lawyer at their side. I have been in this situation on multiple occasions, and lawyers are worth their weight in gold plus more.) Lawyers are not good businesspeople. Like doctors, they are smart, so they think they should be good at business. Not true. One of the hardest things to do in business is to know when to overrule your lawyer and when to listen.

GUT-CHECK YOUR EGO

Can you go to a party with all your old friends and simply be a humble shop owner, or in my case, a barista? If you need people to think you're a big deal, start-up life will be a struggle.

In my business, I see a lot of people who have a hard time simply being the owner of a coffee shop. I hear this line all the time from new owner-operators: "You know, I'm not just going to own one coffee shop. I have plans to open four or five of these stores." Without fail, these people are the ones who never dive in and try to become the best barista, the best single-store operator. But if you don't become a great single-store operator first, it's nearly impossible to become a great five-store operator. True pride knows no shortcuts.

You are going to have to get your nails dirty, and it won't be glamorous for a long time. There aren't going to be a lot of cool stories to share when you get together with friends. You may dread the "So, what do you do?" icebreaker at your spouse's work functions.

Before I started working as a barista, I was a hotshot who sailed around the world, got a great degree from a high-end private college, and made more than $100K my first year out of college in 1993. I had big plans, and coffee was merely a morning beverage. I only started pulling shots of espresso for a little dough before going back to graduate school.

When I eventually became an equal partner in the business, it meant that I got a hearty handshake and a promotion to assistant manager of our only coffee shop. I still had to wear an apron every day, count the pennies, and sweep the floors. My opportunity would only come if the business was successful. The only way the business was going to be successful was if that first store worked. Period.

Not long after I made the decision to bag grad school and pour myself into the coffee business (snort/sigh), an old college friend came back for a visit. He had been wildly successful a few years out of college in the accounting software business. The guy's stock options were worth more than $2 million.

Here I was, making $18,000 a year at a coffee shop, talking about what made our little shop better. Did I believe in my heart that I'd be sitting at a table with him twenty years later having the success I have had? Yes, most certainly. But back then I was happy and excited about making that one single store great. That was all that mattered to me, and I wasn't afraid to proudly describe why to my friend. I knew my future success rested on the foundation of my ability to make that one business successful. I wasn't about to talk hundreds of stores or even tens of stores. I was proud to talk about my one store.

If you aren't ready for this kind of conversation, in which you humble yourself and let people know you have it all on the line— not only money but also your pride and self-worth—you will fail.

I have never understood people who have it all on the line but then don't go all in themselves. If they admit they are all in and it isn't working, then they have to admit they weren't able to make it work, and if they can't make it work, they are a failure. That is hard on the ego. Put your ego in your pocket, or wrap it in cotton and put it in your sock drawer, so that for now you can go all in.

The other trap that comes with worrying about what other people think is the same one that comes with perfectionism: you're avoiding the sales part. That cliché about a great salesman not taking no for an answer applies here. If you're worried about what other people think, then their no's are going to matter to you and beat you down. Can you accept hundreds of no's and wake up tomorrow with the same amount of enthusiasm? All no means is that you didn't do your job well enough. You didn't explain the product fully, because if you had, they would have purchased. No's mean nothing; they don't matter. Get up and keep going.

From my vantage point, I see too many prospective business owners act like they don't need the business or the sale. Someday, maybe, that might be true. But at the beginning, you should beg, bleed, scratch, and claw for every sale, and none of those actions look flattering. Each sale is like wrestling with an alligator while dressed in a suit. Once you've got it pinned down, you have to stand up, flatten out your jacket and tighten your tie, lick down your tussled hair, and carry on like nothing happened. If people laugh and point, you ignore it. Early on I was given more ways why my business wouldn't work than compliments, by a factor of ten. Yet I smiled and kept growing. They simply didn't understand.

Rarely in the start-up phase, if ever, will somebody tell you how wonderful your business is. You can't count on boosts of confidence coming from other people. Rather, you are going to get a ton of "constructive" feedback and criticism. Everyone has an opinion. In addition, all sorts of folks—from your friends and family to really smart lawyers and accountants—will be expecting you to fail. It's not their fault. How else are they supposed to think when almost everyone does?

Tune it out. If you dwell on what they think and say, it's over. Being the founder of a start-up is a lonely place to be, and this is largely why. You have to maintain your belief and confidence, and pound your way through all of the negativity and doubt alone, by yourself. You have to grit your teeth and mumble, "Never mind them; they don't get it!" Other people don't know. They don't understand. How can they? They aren't you. Don't listen to them. What other people think and say simply doesn't matter.

Most people have a hard time admitting that a new business is difficult. As much as you don't want to admit it, your previous successes were often in a contained environment, with great mentors and a support system that was there for you when you needed it. In business for yourself, you are on your own; everything falls on you. There is no legal department to call, no administrative staff to handle your world, and HR isn't on speed dial. This is a hard place to be, and it's often difficult on one's ego. You are responsible for everything, and if it isn't working, the problem is you.

Example: We had a store owned by a family, and it was underperforming. The father called me for lunch. We sat down, and I spent the first twenty minutes listening to his story about life before BIGGBY. He had been the general manager of a $100 million division of one of the largest companies in the world. He talked about his success and how important he was . . . sigh. In his previous life he'd had two—not one, but two—executive assistants.

We finally got around to his business. He was putting the blame squarely on my shoulders for his lack of success. It couldn't have anything to do with him; he was a successful businessman. He understood business. He understood how to manage people. He had been a successful manager of a business. One key factor he was leaving out was that he wasn't responsible for generating the revenue in his prior life. The revenue came in like clockwork. His division sold stuff that was ancillary to the larger company, and as long as he didn't screw it up too badly, the revenue was going to flow. Managing a business like that is like playing checkers. You simply move the parts around the board, and it all works reasonably well in the end.

In a new business, the hardest part is generating the revenue! Since he was already a successful businessman in his mind, he couldn't admit that he didn't know how to engage the business in a way to generate the revenue. His ego was in the way of him admitting he didn't know everything. He couldn't ask for help; in fact, whenever we were together, he spent his time justifying what a great businessman he was as opposed to admitting that maybe we knew a thing or two about selling cups of coffee and we could help.

Ego is powerful. It gets in the way of you learning. It gets in the way of you asking for help. The great proprietors of business get out of their own way, admit they have a ton to learn, and sink themselves in—with their egos in their back pockets.

NAME THE END GAME

The last form of due diligence I advocate is the most important. You must do due diligence on your future. You need to tell me exactly what your future is going to look like in five, ten, twenty years. Not kind of, but exactly what it is going to be like. This is the step most people skip. It is the soft stuff—the mushy stuff nobody pays attention to. Can you imagine if an MBA program included a class on visioning? It is the most important step in planning for your new business. From my experience, the highly successful entrepreneurs have a mechanism for visioning they depend upon. These processes take years to make powerful. MBA classes should be doing a full course on visioning. It has been my secret weapon. It is like magic. If you would like to learn more about our visioning process (it will be the subject of a later book I write), please reach out to me and I will connect you with our resources (517-388-1444).

Why is visioning so important? If you don't know where you are going, if you don't know what the prize is at the end of the journey, you won't stay in the game because the game is too rigorous, too difficult. There are going to be plenty of bad days, when you don't have the energy and enthusiasm you need, when you're sick of being the broke person at the party, when you can't believe you did this to yourself. The best way—perhaps the only way—for you to refrain from curling up in the fetal position and to keep pressing forward is to have the prize so well defined that you can see it, smell it, taste it, touch it. Goals are above bad moods, bad mornings, and bad weeks. You can have all of those, but if you still have your goals, you'll be far more capable of withstanding the pressure and attacks from the boogieman.

Start by writing your end goal down first. It doesn't matter how audacious. In fact, the more obnoxiously unrealistic, the better. Heck, mine is still to own the Detroit Red Wings. That was the goal I set twenty years ago. When I cursed my alarm at four thirty a.m. every Saturday, when I couldn't afford to go on trips with my buddies, when some godforsaken customer missed the toilet. I always knew the price I was paying and for what end—flying on the team plane with the Red Wings to away games.

If I hadn't had the Red Wings in my head, eventually I would've forgotten why I was working as a glorified barista for sixty hours a week. The big goal is my beacon.

You may think an end goal like the Red Wings is too much fantasy to drive you. Really? I love hockey and the Red Wings. They're my passion. They have been my passion for over forty years. What's yours? Do you love fishing? Dining in France? Fast cars? Traveling the world? Curing the disease that killed your mother? Want to retire comfortably before you're sixty? Great. Write it down word for word, send it to me in an email, and then keep it close and read it to yourself every day when you wake up in the morning.

"Obstacles are those frightful things you see when you take your eyes off your goal," Henry Ford famously said. If you don't have goals, you are being led by your circumstance and not by your vision of what the perfect future looks and feels like.

The process I am advocating is much greater and more

powerful than goal setting. Goal setting is part of the work you have to do but is more of a task/accomplishment model. The process I am referring to is visioning. It is about envisioning something you want in the future and spending time connecting with that emotion in the present. People who accomplish great things don't just stumble into great things. They are purposeful and doing some kind of visioning work to make sure their behavior today lines up well with their end game, with their beacon. I don't wake up every day at five a.m. because I don't want to own the Red Wings.

My other audacious goal is to be active until I am one hundred years old. Today, I have worked out every day in succession for over 1,400 days. I want to enjoy my children and their children. In order to live a full life and to be with them on their journey, I have to make it to one hundred. I believe exercise is fundamental to longevity. Therefore, I am acting today on how I want my life to look in the future.

It doesn't have to be grandiose visions like owning the Red Wings or living to one hundred years old. Visioning applies to the everyday, too.

Example: Three months prior to meeting my wife, I was in a bad place. I was miserable, and I wanted a family, a home, a partner. My brother sat me down and told me to put my preaching about visioning to work. He told me to give him every detail about the future wife I wanted. We created a list; on it were eighteen characteristics, and I referred to the list almost daily. All of a sudden dating became pretty simple. If I met a woman who didn't match up well with my list, she wasn't somebody I was going to make an investment in.

On my second date with my now wife, I realized that she had seventeen and a half out of those eighteen characteristics. I knew at that moment I was going to marry her. Sounds crazy, and I wouldn't believe it if it didn't happen to me. I have many more examples, but the truth of the matter is that you have to keep your eyes focused on your destination so the body shots you take along the way are understood as what they are: minor obstacles in getting to your end goal.

Nobody ever accomplished anything worthwhile without wanting it really, really badly. What do you want? Figure it out, and then remind yourself every day of what it is. Tape it to the mirror in your bathroom next to the Socrates quote. Put it on the inside flap of your wallet. Tape it to your rearview mirror.

At some point in the process, you will begin feeling comfortable sharing your goal. This is when things become truly powerful. Now you are enlisting other people in helping reach your goals. Today, I hear about the Red Wings regularly. I am not ashamed of my ambition. I am proud of it. I am up to something. People love to talk about it and support me. Set your goal and start working. People will ask what you are up to, and your answer will be amazingly powerful.

Craig Silverstein, Google's first employee, tells a story about offhandedly setting ridiculously high expectations/goals: "I would joke that maybe one day we will, like, have a million dollars in revenue, and Sergey was like, 'A million? No, a billion.'"[6]

Now that you have your ridiculously ambitious end goal, it's time to break it up into stages or steps. I didn't wake up

6   *Bloomberg Game Changers*, "Sergey Brin and Larry Page," YouTube link no longer available.

this morning and go to work thinking that what I am doing today is going to make owning the Red Wings a reality. I may be slightly delusional, but I have some roots in reality. You have to take the big one and make it incremental. You have to understand how today and tomorrow are leading to the Big Harry Audacious one.[7]

At my stage today, I know the next step in my development is to be the dominant gourmet coffee retailer in the Great Lakes region. National dominance doesn't happen unless you become regionally dominant. And I don't have a shot at owning the Red Wings unless we have a nationally dominant brand of coffee shops. You don't "will" yourself to a national retail chain. You reach millions of incremental steps, millions of goals and milestones along the way. You have to set them, accomplish them, and move on to the next set of goals. One day you will wake up and think, *Holy crap, I might have a chance at making this goal work.* You are now empowered.

Here is my example from sports. You can't talk about goals without a sports story. One of our franchisees, Kip Miller, was a great college hockey player who won the Hobey Baker Award, which is college hockey's Heisman Trophy. From the time he was seven years old, he wanted to play in the pros (like every other kid who ever played a sport). He didn't go into his first year of college hockey at Michigan State University with the idea of making the pros or being the best college hockey player in the country. He simply wanted to score seventeen goals. Then his sophomore year, he wanted to score twenty-two. It

---

7   Jim Collins and Jerry I. Porras, *Built to Last* (New York: William Collins, 2004.)

was all incremental in his head, and he stayed focused on his next milestone. The larger goals came to fruition, but only because he was able to reach each of the next markers he had set for himself. The larger goal, playing in the pros, was always there as a beacon, but he obsessed over his short-term markers.

There are two things to point out about this. First, every decision you make in the start-up phase is either in line with your end goal or it isn't. If it isn't, I think you know the result. Second, not everyone has to know about your wild and crazy dream at the beginning. In fact, most people shouldn't know, at first. Keep it to yourself for a while, and let it be your internal fire. There will be a moment you will share it with the world, but at the beginning you don't want to come across as half-cocked or crazy.

THE POWERFUL STUFF IS SIMPLE

You don't pick up the knowledge you need to make the decisions that will truly impact the overall success of your business in business school. You gain it from your parents, your third-grade teacher, your grandparents, your best friend in middle school, and all the struggles you've already overcome to get to right now, the present.

In my experience, the most successful people are good people. When you look at the men and women who do amazing things in entrepreneurship, they're usually decent, honest, hardworking people. Their intentions are to be good people, and their drive is innate. You learn those lessons early in life. They are developed in your upbringing.

I had a student come up to me and say, "I never knew someone could be so successful and also be a nice guy and care about his people." It was one of the best compliments I've ever received. It's not about being a genius. It isn't quantitative. What it is about is maintaining the right attitude, staying focused on your goal, and being good to people day in and day out.

The things that have worked for me are the simple ones. I make my bed every morning. I work hard and study. I truly think about the other person in every situation, how they are doing, how they are feeling. There's no way I'll ever be the smartest person, but I can control my attitude and how I treat people. From my experience, if people think you're a good person—if your enthusiasm is infectious, you work your ass off, you show up, and are dependable—they want to help you.

It all sounds pretty easy. And on the page, it looks easy. I agree. But being able to honestly examine yourself—to admit your faults, identify your shortcomings, and have laser-like focus on what is important—is extremely difficult. In my experience, few people consider the importance of doing true due diligence on themselves: being self-aware and understanding if they have what it takes.

You are the key ingredient in the success of your start-up. Optimizing you starts with knowing your own strengths and weaknesses. Once you understand those, you can begin to compensate and put together a dynamic, high-functioning team to launch your new business to its first day of positive cash flow.

Chapter 2

SELL MORE SHIT!

HERE COMES THE NUMBER ONE piece of advice I can give you in your new start-up. Wake up tomorrow and figure out how to sell more shit. The natural tendency is to bolt on more complexity, add more products, tweak your current lineup of product. You know your core product, so spend all of your time obsessing over new and different ways to sell your core product, to sell more shit. Period.

Cash is the lifeblood of your start-up. There is absolutely no time to waste when it comes to generating revenue. Once you've quit your job, invested your nest egg, and secured that initial loan, the meter starts running. It is now a race: the gun has gone off and you are sprinting to get revenue high enough to have the gross margin that gives you one dollar left over after you have paid both your variable and fixed expenses. That is our goal, our finish line; that is our everything for this book. It is that simple.

This is the part everyone, and I mean everyone, underestimates. Revenue is very difficult to find. This is why most businesses fail. In my business we have had to fight for every dollar we generate. There wasn't one dollar that came easy; not one.

Why, then, is revenue the most important part of your start-up? Because after you have opened your doors for business, for most of you it is going to be your only source of cash to keep your business operational.

You are open, negative cash flowing, bleeding: you are in the red. You have used up every dime of cash you have, and money is hard to find, unless you have a rich uncle. But in my experience, rich uncles aren't that easy, either. Besides, who wants to spend the family gatherings avoiding the rich uncle, who is now drunk and wants to know how his money is doing? The only source of cash is revenue coming in your "door."

The point I want to hammer home in this chapter is that revenue is harder to get than you think. A lot harder. So what are you going to do about it?

Spend as little time as possible planning the "how" it is going to happen, and get going on making it happen. I am writing a book on business start-ups, and I want you to take note that I completely skipped any section about planning. No need to spend a month of your life getting the business plan perfect. No point in figuring out exit strategies or capitalization tables with different layers of debt structured for the eventual liquidity event. This stuff is silly.

I heard recently from a manager at a private equity firm that they are recommending start-ups present a one-page outline of their marketing plan. They don't want to see your revenue forecast, and they don't want to see your initial investment detailed down to the penny. They simply want to see how you intend to sell product and generate revenue. If you can convince them you know how to turn your product into cash in the bank, not even how much cash, they may be willing to invest. I love this. This is one of the smartest things I have ever heard from an investor. If you think you can predict how the consumer is going to react to your new business, and therefore you think you know how much of your product you are going to sell, you are naïve. Launch with your one-page marketing plan, execute, and adapt based on customer response. It really is that simple. Eric Reis has done a great job explaining this theory in his book, *The Lean Startup.*

When we were starting to expand BIGGBY beyond its initial two stores, I went to about fifteen family friends—close friends—and pitched them our investment opportunity. I was only able to secure four meetings, and I got no's from all four. This response caught me off guard, frankly. It even hurt a little. I thought, knowing them as well as I did, that they would've believed in me, and in our idea, and invested. I wasn't even trying to raise a lot of money—only about $50,000 total. But they weren't buying. Not a one.

What I learned is that money, and the people who have it, is smart. Most people who have means have systems in place to make sure they don't give any of it to a twenty-four-year-old kid with ridiculous dreams of a coffee shop empire. When I approached them, they inevitably suggested that I meet with "their guy," who was typically a professional money manager. These guys are smart, and there's no way they're going to advise their clients—my family friends—to invest with me.

When you're a start-up founder, you quickly run into a nasty catch-22 that can be hard to overcome. The best time to get money, whether it's from your family and friends or a bank, is before your business launches. This is when it's just an idea full of hope and promise, and there aren't any negative cash flow statements or balance sheets.

You have a chance in the "idea phase" to convince them that you're going to do well, and while it's extremely tough to close a deal with investors at any stage, the business's potential is still a selling point. Once you launch, it gets more difficult, because now you've got real numbers, and let's face it, they're in the red. Businesses that open and do well enough to positive cash flow in the first six to nine months are few and far between. I like to refer to these situations as lottery winners. It might happen, it could happen, and I certainly hope it does, but you can't plan on it. It would be the same as planning your retirement on simply winning the lottery. That's about as foolish as opening and expecting your business to cash flow in its first year.

So: you are open for business, you aren't doing revenue, you are negative cash flowing, you are out of money. This leaves you with two options to keep your business going:

1. **Infuse equity**: You can beg, borrow, and steal cash. There are credit cards; you may have close friends who are willing to give you a personal loan as charity. Frankly, when you are hurting for cash, it is almost impossible to find a new source of cash.

2. **Sell more core product**: Most often, this is the only answer. If you don't figure out how to start generating revenue, you're sunk. Being the greatest salesperson in the world needs to take 80 percent of your attention and focus.

#*&% SELLING

Let me blow you away with a statistic from *The Origin and Evolution of New Businesses* by Amar Bhide: 75 percent of the CEOs on the Inc. 500 list of fastest-growing companies considered themselves to be the primary or only salesperson in the business at start-up. I think one of the reasons is that only 10 percent of this group had MBAs.[1] Not that there is anything wrong with an MBA—MBAs are great if you are planning on managing a business that has an established revenue stream. I think they lack when it comes to the art of selling. Entrepreneurship is about creating that revenue stream. I have watched hundreds of hours of videos on entrepreneurship from amazing institutions like Stanford and Harvard. I never came across a presentation on selling: the importance of waking up in the morning and cold calling, the importance of the art of closing the deal, the funnel as a sales mechanism, the importance of generating leads, how to generate leads, etc.

I saw presentations on the top ten things to do when making a presentation to a venture capital firm. I saw all kinds of research and presentations on the value chain. In my research, I learned all about corporate culture and governance. Not once did I come across a book on entrepreneurship that advocated

---

1   Amar V. Bhide, *The Origin and Evolution of New Businesses* (Oxford University Press, 2003).

the top ten most effective ways to make a sale or build a process for selling product. It is as though if you do everything else right, revenue will take care of itself. If you remember one thing from this book, please remember this: revenue does not take care of itself! Are you willing to call yourself a salesperson? Are you willing to say that your primary job in the business is selling? My assumption here is most people graduating with an MBA are not willing to refer to themselves as the sales rep for their business. They are the manager, the CEO, but there is nothing to manage if you aren't a hardcore salesperson first.

From one proprietor to another, from a guy who doesn't have an MBA, who bootstrapped his business, who is still bootstrapping his business even though he is selling over $100 million a year in product: revenue is the most important part of your start-up. Period. Yet most people avoid sales like the plague.

> I have met many servicemen about to go to war. I also have met many entrepreneurs about to go into business. It would appear that the fledgling entrepreneur is more scared of selling than the soldier is of fighting. How on earth can the fear of rejection be greater than that of bullets and bombs?[2]

So why are you so terrified to sell?

People are scared of rejection. People are forced to put their egos in their pocket when they are selling. When you are

---

2   Alex McMillan, *Be a Great Entrepreneur* (Hodder & Stoughton, 2010).

selling, you are constantly being told what is wrong with your product and company, and therefore you are being told what is wrong with you.

I think it comes down to people thinking and believing that the salesman is the lowest common denominator in business. The salesman is the cheesy guy or the flirtatious girl who didn't have the grades to get into business college or accounting. They get by on their good looks and charming personality, not on their business acumen.

Also, people are afraid of accountability. In sales, you are either selling product or not. There is no hiding. If you are in the accounting department or in logistics, as long as your boss likes you, most likely your job is safe. In sales you post your number every month. How many sales did you make? There is no excuse. This is the same reason golf is an infuriating game to many people. You go out on a course and you post a score. There is nobody to blame but yourself. In sales, like golf, you post a number; if it is a good number you win, and if it is a bad number you lose. It is up to you and only you.

I think it comes down to people not wanting to work hard. A good salesman works really hard. It is repetitive; it is boring. You must be super disciplined. It is a ton of simple math and small numbers that add up to a bunch of hard work and in the end, you certainly hope, to a bunch of big numbers. You make forty phone calls in a day, you schedule eight appointments on average, and you make a sale every twelve and a half appointments. If you need four sales a month, you'd better figure out how to make 160 sales calls per month. That is not simple and it is not fun, but it is how you will make your business successful.

OK, OK, OK . . . Mike, I get it. Sales is important; it is the only thing that matters in a start-up. I've bought in, but how?

THE REVENUE-GENERATING MIND-SET

The revenue mind-set is one that is perfectly focused on the customer. If you are obsessed with generating more revenue, you are obsessed with the customer. If the customer has the perfect experience, one of three things is going to happen: (1) They are going to spend more money with you the next time they are with you, (2) They are going to come back and see you more often, or (3) They are going to promote your business to their friends and family. Point three is the most critical component to the revenue-generating mind-set. How you grow revenue and grow revenue quickly is getting your customers to become promoters of your business. Promoters create exponential growth in sales.

You only do this by providing them the perfect experience so they fall in love with you and your brand; then you have to ask them to promote you to their friends and family. I know, you know, everyone knows when they are in love with a brand. You have a great feeling when associated with the brand. You are that brand, and that brand is you. My son can't comprehend why anyone would buy a Pepsi. He has always been a Coke guy. If he sees someone drinking a Pepsi, he will scoff, roll his eyes, and act like there has been a grave injustice. A friend of mine in college had a bumper sticker on his Chevy truck, with Calvin from *Calvin and Hobbes* peeing on the Ford logo. You have to work hard every minute to turn people into fanatics of your brand. They will promote you; they will defend you. The power of brand loyalty is amazing. You have to be willing to ask people to actively engage in promoting you. One of the lines I used to love using in my stores was, "Don't forget I am a for-profit business; if you love our coffee, if you love our business, make sure to tell your friends and family about us." Americans love a hustler: they love the guy who is trying really hard or the gal who is hell-bent on succeeding. America loves a climber.

Many people believe advertising and promotion are the answers to generating revenue. But dollars spent on advertising and promotion are a waste if they generate a fresh face for your business and that fresh face has a moderate experience. People don't become loyal to a business—they don't become promoters—based on moderate or mediocre experiences. Until you have the experience perfectly figured out, don't waste your time or money on advertising or promotion. It is like burning crisp, clean $100 bills.

What are the *three critical components* of creating a culture in your business of obsessing over sales, otherwise known as obsessing over the customer experience?

SET THE TONE, PAY FULL PRICE

When customers, vendors, friends, and even my own mother come into my business while I'm working, I will never let them pull me away from what I am doing. I am working the business, I am engaged, I am making it happen. I am selling more product.

When a friend or my mom stops in, I give a big hug and I'm back to work. When a sales rep wants to meet, I do it standing up for six minutes max, and then I'm back to work. The salesperson leaves with a full-price drink, I promise. My mother pays full price. I might buy a drink for her, but I pull out my credit card and pay full price. This is a critical management point to be addressed in a later book, but for this book, making my mom pay full price is about maximizing my revenue that hour. I always want to maximize revenue every hour of every day. It is a game to me; we are constantly in a battle to beat the previous hour.

If somebody—a friend or your mother—walks into your business and is offended because you are asking them to pay full price, they aren't your friend. If they see you pull out your wallet and pay for the product yourself, it will have impact. In uncomfortable situations, I always defer to my partners by saying, "I don't think my partner would like to buy half of your coffee, considering they don't even know you." Then I laugh, smile, and move on.

Another tactic is upselling. Every business has upselling tactics, ways of generating more revenue per customer. When I am working, I am deploying these upselling tools perfectly. I am procedurally sound. I set the example that the procedures are important. They are to be used every time without exception. In my business, upselling is as simple as asking if they would like a blueberry muffin this morning. Ask the customer if they want a larger size. Whatever the upsell mechanism of the day is, use it yourself, show people how it is done. If you don't use it, neither will they.

SELL EVERY MINUTE

Also, I am ruthless with my time. I am committed to making sure that every available minute I have is obsessively focused on selling. There isn't one second to waste.

Eighty percent of your daily work in the first year of your business should be dedicated to making that one additional sale. This is difficult, even impossible, to do without setting a strict schedule to keep you on task. This work is usually routine, monotonous work. It is twenty cold calls a day with follow-up calls to boot. You end up leaving thirty-seven voice mails out of forty calls you make over two days. Out of the three people you talk to, you get two no's and one person who is considering your product. There you have it: one person considering your product.

In my world, it is standing behind an espresso machine six hours a day. No cell phone, no interruptions, just waiting to focus on that one new customer who is going to walk in my store and provide me the opportunity to turn them into a fanatic of my business. It is sitting and handwriting twenty cards to people you met at a chamber of commerce event. Sure, you could send an email, but a handwritten card shows real effort, and effort opens doors. It is like personally calling somebody back who came through your 1-800 number or who sent feedback electronically on the website.

Here is an example of my daily schedule when we first started BIGGBY:

5:00 a.m.   Arrive fifteen minutes before everyone else, turn lights on, and get the coffee brewing.

5:55 a.m.   Turn the open sign on and open for business (this is a big deal every morning—300 seconds early).

6:00 a.m.   Make espresso drinks, no interruptions, no meetings, no phone calls.

11:00 a.m.   Prepare cash and sales data sheet from previous day; walk the money to the bank.

12:00 p.m.   Make espresso drinks; check in with staff to make sure everything was completed for the shift change.

1:00 p.m.   Work on guerilla marketing, both tactically and from an execution perspective.

2:45 p.m.   Be available to jump up on the floor whenever the 3:00 p.m. rush arrives.

3:30 p.m.   Work on administrative tasks (ordering, scheduling, hiring, etc.); as soon as I am done, I can go home.

Notice that I scheduled myself on the floor, with an apron on, running the cash register for six hours a day. That is not a typo. I dedicated six hours a day to a job that I pay someone a little more than minimum wage to do. I wasn't in the back placing orders or doing payroll. I wasn't standing off to the side meeting with vendors. None of that stuff was going to get me closer to positive cash flow. Ringing up and taking orders from customers was my answer. Administrative work doesn't grow the business. What tactics are you going to deploy to grow your business?

Setting up my schedule so I could be on the floor six hours a day had two essential results:

1. It helped me connect with the business in a fundamental way. I was able to see exactly what my customers and employees saw. Not only could I set an example for my staff (more on that in a moment), but I was able to see—even feel—what customers were responding to and attracted by, so I could do more to enhance those things later. This is invaluable information that you would never get by holing up in the back or just popping in to check on things. Plus, it's invigorating to see new customers discover the business you've created. Don't deny yourself that little daily dose of satisfaction, as it's a powerful motivator, especially during the highly uncertain start-up phase.

2. It forced me to be more efficient with my time and do the administrative stuff like ordering and payroll in a short window. Let's face it, this is the crappy grunt work anyway. It didn't allow me to waste away hours procrastinating when I needed to be out front with the customers. Also, why spend your whole day doing the stuff that isn't fun? Bang out the necessary administrative evils in two hours and go home. I would purposefully put it at the end of the day because the sooner you get through this stuff, the sooner you can go home and relax.

This six-hour rule is so important that we require each BIGGBY owner-operator to be out front in their store six hours a day for the first year. We actually write it into the contract.

If you are this committed to selling, if you are maniacal about selling, everyone in your organization will see it, and it will cascade throughout the organization. You are setting the tone that sales revenue is the most important thing within the company. A sales culture is what you are trying to create, and if you don't set the tone, you won't have one—and your days in business will be numbered.

EVERYONE SELLS

If you are working within the company and you have the opportunity to engage and interact with the customer, then you have the opportunity to help grow the business. If you have the opportunity to turn someone into a promoter, then you have the opportunity to sell. Turning your customers into promoters of your business is sales. Yes, even if you are in accounting, you have the opportunity to sell. How in the world does somebody in accounts receivable have the opportunity to sell?

Let me give you an example from my life. I work with a car dealership here in Ann Arbor called Germain. I had confusion with my last car purchase. My car had serious issues the first evening I drove it. They did the right thing and replaced the car, upgrading me to the premium package at no additional charge. This all sounds simple—just swap out the cars. But I realized three or four weeks later that the bank had the wrong VIN number associated with my loan. They had the VIN number for the original car, not the new one. Again, it doesn't sound like a big deal, but if you are dealing with a bank, then it becomes a big deal very quickly. Of course, the bank had to verify the VIN number was accurate, and they reached out to the dealership's accounting department.

This is a great example of how accounting can sell, a great example of a selling culture. Somebody from the accounting department reached out to me and apologized for the inconvenience, saying they should have updated the bank with the new VIN number. They were going to handle everything, and they would keep me posted. They had to call me a couple of times to ask me questions and had me call the bank to fill in some information. They gave me a direct number to a person with a real name. It was simple for me, and I appreciated their engagement. Two weeks later, I got a phone call from the woman in accounting, who wanted to make sure everything had worked out and I didn't have any more issues. It felt like a family member or a close friend was taking care of me, and she was from accounting. I have told multiple people about how great "my" dealership is, and you can bet your tuchus that I will be buying at least my next five cars from them. One woman in accounting turned me from a satisfied customer to a dead loyal customer, and to a promoter of their business.

Everyone in the business who interacts with the customer is selling. Even those who may not have the opportunity to interact with the customer can sell by supporting those who do, or they can make observations about processes or procedures that don't seem to be working for the customer. For example, somebody in accounts receivable can send a nice card to a customer thanking them for paying on time and being such a great partner. How many times have you heard of that happening?

For start-ups to be successful, they have to build a selling culture from day one. Selling isn't something you learn to do later; you have to build the culture before you open your doors. If it isn't a part of the culture from the beginning, you are going to struggle to grow revenue quickly enough to get to (+)cash flow before it is too late.

ONE NEW SALES IDEA PER WEEK

You have your advertising and promotional campaign in full force when you open. By advertising and promotion, I am referring to the big levers: digital media, radio, television, and outdoor. I am also referring to having a PR firm on retainer grinding away at getting your campaign seen by as many people as possible. This is the easy stuff. No big deal—decide on your campaign, lock in six- to twelve-month contracts, and let it roll. This way, you don't think about it again. You lock this stuff in place before you open, you have your budget allocated, you have decided what to buy, and it is now a machine working in the background. You shouldn't play with your advertising and promotional campaign more than quarterly. Now what?

Assemble your team, pull out a yellow legal pad circa 1998, and tell them you want to hear every possible idea or thought they can conjure to help generate more revenue. In my business we call this guerrilla marketing: the things we do to generate interest, generate traffic to our door that is not one of the major levers. Get together with your team—everyone—quarterly and brainstorm. Your people are in the business every day, the same as you are, and they see opportunities for revenue generation as well. Develop the list of ideas. Organize your list, and then present it to the group and have the group vote and prioritize the list based on votes. Assign one task per week over the next quarter. Assign responsibilities and then execute. Get together three months later, talk about what worked and what didn't, and do it all over again. This process is magical! Why?

One, you get ideas from people who are in the middle of it every day! They are engaged with the customer, they know the customer, and they see and feel the struggles the customers are having with your business. They have to be involved in this process if you want to have the customer sitting at the table when you are figuring out how to get the customer to love your business and buy more from you. Two, if the ideas are everyone's ideas, then your people will buy in because they see and feel that they are getting to engage the business in a meaningful way. Then they will actually execute what the group decides.

If the ideas come from and are mandated by the "top," they will mostly be ignored. From my experience, people are more inspired to execute when they were involved in creating what is going to be executed. Getting everyone involved in one sales idea per week is critical to its success, and one new idea per week is critically important to the success of your business. Why is this so important? Top-down ideas are doomed for failure in sales because if they work, the leader gets the credit, and if they fail, the staff has no responsibility.

Every month, every week, every day, you and your entire team need to be actively engaged in selling. Active engagement is crucial; the act of engaging is how everyone in your universe knows you are going to succeed, that there is no option other than success. At the beginning during start-up, you must be intentional, and methodic—in my opinion, once a week.

Your weekly meeting has to be in bright yellow on your calendar. You have to do it every single week; never miss. You have to plan it out. This grassroots-type stuff—guerrilla marketing, if you want to call it that—during the start-up phase is so crucial. Don't skip a week. Report out on successes; report out on failures. Talk, work, sell, analyze, talk, work, sell, analyze. Every week. You will get better and better as the weeks go by. Unfortunately during start-up, this meeting—if it is even scheduled—is the first one to get blown off. It doesn't feel urgent. There is always a reason not to do it. But this one meeting, if executed, will be the single most powerful meeting on your calendar. Do it religiously. You can't do it sporadically. It can't be something you work on when everything else is done. It has to be your primary focus. It has to be your obsession.

COST CUTTING IS THE SILVER BULLET

What mistakes do people make? What gets in the way of new proprietors obsessing over revenue? It is so important! Why would anything get in the way of selling? Because there is an easier way to profit: cost cutting.

People make rash decisions when they're short on cash, and generally everyone is short on cash in start-up. It's just human nature. Usually, the first thing people do in this situation is to start cutting costs. This is a mistake. I have seen too many people give up right before they were about to see positive cash flow. Their focus gets pulled away from generating revenue and toward saving money. Once you start down this road, you might as well dust off your resume and go to Plan B. Cost savings are a one-time event. If you cut fifty dollars today, you're going to have to do it again tomorrow to get the same effect. You'll always have to be cutting until there's nothing left.

Labor cost is the first thing start-up owners look at when they get nervous and start looking to cut corners. Most often, this ends up being an incredibly short-sighted decision that almost never mitigates damage.

Recently, I was sitting with a group of new owner-operators discussing labor management. They were wondering whether they should have two or three people on during the morning shift. Many in the room had already gone down to two baristas, and, in my opinion, service levels were suffering.

I did the math. They had, on average, $250,000 invested in the business. They were struggling, and having that third person for six hours a day cost them between $13k and $15k, in 2008 dollars, per year! They weren't willing to spend the extra fourteen grand to provide the service level necessary to ramp up sales? That didn't make any sense, and it was because they were looking at labor as an expense and a method of cost mitigation rather than as an asset and a tool for revenue expansion. This is one of the simplest concepts in this book—but one I see almost everyone who is struggling get wrong.

The other popular line item that's first to get slashed is the advertising and marketing budget. Really? So you're struggling to generate positive cash flow in your start-up and you want to *decrease* the chances of potential customers finding out about you? Remember my advice from earlier. Lock in your advertising and promotional campaign for your first year, and don't think about it again. Be bold, be consistent, and you will find your advertising and promotional dollars working for you.

Also, be wary of getting caught up in the tiny details. Selling is hard. Generating revenue is hard. So hard, in fact, that a lot of times people can end up focusing on cutting the minuscule stuff to feel like they've accomplished something. This can be a psychological trap, however, that makes you feel like you're still trying to make the business work while also avoiding the most difficult—and yet most crucial—part of a successful start-up: revenue generation, sales.

Take my "parfait berries story" for example. At BIGGBY, we put a strawberry and a half at the bottom of our yogurt parfaits. It looks great and tastes even better. Six months into his operation, a BIGGBY operator calls me up and says strawberry prices are "just absurd." The price was indeed fluctuating like crazy, I'll give him that. So he tells me he wants to switch to blueberries. Great, I say, and then I do the math. I quickly figure out it'll save him about $1.50 to $2.00 a week. I'm not kidding. This new operator is not generating positive cash flow, and instead of being out there greeting new customers and providing them an experience that will turn them into a promoter of the business, he's sitting in the back trying to think of ways he can save a few bucks a week on yogurt parfaits when our core product is lattes and drip coffee. How much time and energy was spent just trying to save one, two, even three dollars a week? If he got only one person to come back and buy another caramel latte a week, he'd make more money. Yet it was easier for him to be in the back trying to shave off expenses than out front selling more coffee drinks.

It's worth repeating: each cost-cutting move is finite. You save that dollar you just saved and only that dollar. In order for it to be effective, you have to keep finding one more cut. Once you start that process of cutting, it's hard to stop. And when you are focused on cutting, you're not focused on revenue generation, and each decision that follows will take you a few more degrees off course. On the flip side, generating one new regular and turning them into a promoter of your business has a compounding effect. That new customer will be back many more times and generate revenue for years and years, and more importantly, they will bring somebody back with them.

FOCUS ON THE CUSTOMER

This shift in mentality is core-level stuff. It is the backbone of this chapter and the basis for chapter 4. When you're focused on revenue, you're focused on the customer experience. In trying to generate cash flow, you're automatically going to be focused on trying to make sure customers come back tomorrow. When you get obsessed with costs, you begin to neglect the customer. It's that simple.

A challenge I give to operators to hammer this concept home is: "If I offered you seven hundred dollars today to go out and create one new regular customer, could you do it?" Seven hundred dollars is about the average amount a regular customer will spend in one of our stores per year. To a person, they all say, "Hell yeah, I could do that."

It sounds easy, yet most people don't break it down to the simple goal of trying to generate one new customer a day. If they did, however, in one year they'd have 365 regular customers in their business and it would be successful. It astonishes me how many people in most businesses don't understand how simple this concept is. Instead, they focus on the minutiae—like parfait berries—that are not material to the business.

AVOID THE ADMINISTRATIVE CYCLONE

I mentioned the trap of getting caught up in the meaningless minutiae to avoid selling and to make you feel like you're still moving the business forward. This is worth discussing in more depth.

I can't stress enough how important it is to leave all but the necessary administrative stuff behind. That includes meetings, conversations and small talk, email, spreadsheet analysis, and the like. Think I'm being a little extreme? You only have so many hours in each day to get things done. A twenty-minute conversation here, a ten-minute conversation there, and all of a sudden you've wasted 10 percent of your time that day on things that haven't resulted in a single sale.

Some math: there are six hundred minutes in a ten-hour workday. You are already spending 360 of those minutes on barista duties and 120 minutes on administrative work, so you have 120 minutes left to promote your business. You have one fifteen-minute meaningless conversation; add another ten-minute one and a five-minute one, and you have burned thirty minutes. That is 25 percent of the time you allocated to selling. This is exactly how people erode time needed for selling. Add this up over a week or a month, and then tell me how extreme I'm being. The two hours on selling have to be protected.

When you're at work and not selling, you should be focusing on and 100 percent committed to providing the most extraordinary customer experience possible in order to create as many promoters as possible.

Example: One of the best examples I can think of comes from a family-run restaurant called Halls Chophouse in gorgeous Charleston, South Carolina. My wife and I were there for a long weekend getaway. All dressed up for a night out, we walked into the packed restaurant, and before we could even get to the host stand to check in, a guy in a suit walks up to us and says, "You're the McFall party." He turns to my wife and asks, "Are you Elizaveta? Thank you for coming. Your table is ready, but I've saved two seats at the bar for you. Why don't you just sit down, relax, and enjoy a drink, and when you are ready I will take you to your table for dinner. You are sitting at one of my favorite tables in the entire restaurant. Just let me know." Then he brings his brother over and introduces him to us. My wife leans in and whispers, "Do they think we're someone we're not?" I watch this owner do the same thing with most people, in one way or another, all night long.

As we're leaving, he comes back over, shakes our hands, wishes us a nice trip, and says, "I can't wait to see you the next time you're in Charleston."

Since that trip a few years ago, my wife and I have talked

about Halls Chophouse and how unbelievable the experience was a hundred times. There is no doubt that when we are back in Charleston, we will return. Heck, we've even talked about taking another trip there just so we can have that dining experience again!

He wasn't in the back, making sure the steaks were coming out the right temperature. He wasn't watching whether the bartenders were overpouring. He was out front, making sure that every single one of his customers was having a memorable experience. In his business, if he can't rely on someone to cook his steaks properly or make an old fashioned, he's in big trouble.

In a start-up, you have to farm out all of the simple tasks that only require proper execution, and you have to find a way to do it fast. Someone else can cook the steaks medium rare. Someone else can write the weekly work schedule or put in the Sysco order. These are binary processes. If you're down to three bottles of vanilla syrup and you typically stock seven, then order four. You can pay someone minimum wage to do that math.

Many new business owners I see consider the important stuff to be writing the schedule and counting the cash drawer. Ego comes in. They want to own a BIGGBY, but they don't want to make the coffee. Making the coffee during start-up is the only way. Make it perfect, make it fast, every time, and let someone else do the fourth-grade math to place an order or write a schedule. Former engineers and accountants, especially, like checklists. Being out front and dealing with the customer is not a checkable item, yet it's the most important thing you can do as a start-up owner.

Give up the administration so you can focus on the customer.

PITFALLS

There are entire books devoted to the pitfalls of starting a new business. Frankly, I think that's a bit too much negativity for people who are just getting started. Devoting part of a chapter to some key pitfalls, however, seems more appropriate.

Blame Game: It can't be your fault, because you are perfect

It's so easy to find excuses for why your business isn't working that it's an eye-rolling cliché. Again, you don't want to be a cliché. If revenue is slow, it's your fault. Pull your pants up and fix it. I'm quoting none other than my mom on this one. Growing up, she always used to tell me, "Make the decision, and then work your butt off to make sure the decision you made was the right one." You went into business. Now get out there and sell enough product to make the business work.

Any time you spend trying to justify why things aren't working is simply wasting energy that you could be using to figure out how to sell more product. One of the great business quotes of all time was by Estée Lauder: "If the product doesn't sell, it isn't the product's fault." Here are some examples of excuses you shouldn't waste time with:

· "The economy is bad." Get over it. It's bad for everyone.

· "My location isn't as visible as it could be." Then be more creative with your imaging.

· "A competitor came into our space and . . ." Really? You want to admit that you flat-out got beat?

· "The weather has been horrific this year." So now it's Mother Nature's fault?

· "It's so hard to find good help." That's probably because good workers don't want to work for someone who's always making excuses.

Like in life, you can always find reasons why things aren't working. Your job is to find the answers to generate revenue and make it work.

I can't tell you how many times I've heard people talk about why their businesses aren't working. I usually cut these conversations short. I don't have time to listen to excuses, and you shouldn't have time to make them. You have a new business to run! So do I!

These conversations aren't focused on making the business work. Instead, every time you open your mouth to complain, it sounds an alarm that the business is in trouble, and nobody wants to do business with someone who is going broke. Once you are in the downward death spiral of negativity it is almost impossible to pull yourself out.

To quote our biggest owner-operator, Mohamed Shetiah, who at the time of this writing has twenty-four stores, "When something goes wrong, don't find someone to blame. Fix it!"

Not going all in

This seems pretty obvious. If you're going to start a new business, of course you're going to give it all you have, right? Not necessarily. It's easy to slow down at the first signs of trouble, and it may not even be a conscious decision. It is easy to stay focused when things are going great, when the phone is ringing off the hook or there is a line of customers to the door. The real challenge is to stay focused and give it 100 percent when the business is middling.

Expectations are powerful beasts. Most people I interact with during or before start-up have wildly misaligned expectations. In many ways I think people need to have unrealistic expectations about the performance of their new business in order to do it in the first place. The problem is that when the business comes out of the gate slowly, there is a disappointment, and if you don't have great resolve, this can be the beginning of the end.

Nobody wants to be a failure. And for some, that first taste of disappointment can start to breed apathy, because, well, if you don't give it your all, then when things fail, at least you can tell yourself, "It would have worked if I had just put in more effort." There's something easier about admitting that you were lazy than admitting that you tried with all of your heart and you still failed. People let pride and ego get in the way of their own success. I am sure there is a psychological syndrome that leads to this behavior, as it has real impact on people's behavior.

Sometimes going all in is not glamorous. I was wearing an apron and pulling espresso shots for my buddies who came in to give me a hard time before they went to play eighteen holes on a gorgeous Saturday morning. I mopped the floor every day. Yet those are the times I look back on now and see as the main reasons why everything worked in the end. Now that my business is infinitely more complex, these are the things I long for. I wish it were as simple as standing there being 100 percent present while pulling shots of espresso or making sure the floor got mopped perfectly or the open sign got turned on three hundred seconds before open.

Second, and maybe most importantly, there is some magic in going all in. When you give something 100 percent of your effort, when you are obsessed with an outcome, willing to do whatever it takes, you unlock and give yourself permission to succeed.

By the time I was a junior in college, I had tried to qualify for the Michigan Amateur golf tournament a few times and had missed the cut. I made a commitment to myself that I wanted to try as hard as I could; I wanted to give it 100 percent. I needed to go all in. I was fortunate to be living with my parents for a few months leading up to the qualifier. I announced to my friends and family what I would be doing. They were supportive, as they knew it was a relatively short-term focus for something I really wanted to accomplish.

Monday through Friday I was working as an intern in the sales office of a golf resort. My boss was an avid golfer, so she too was supportive of the work I was doing at the golf course. Every weekday, I was up and at the practice range at my boyhood haunt, Dunham Hills Golf Course, by five o'clock a.m. I had worked there throughout high school; the owners and most of the employees were friends. I told them what I was doing, and they got behind me, too. We had it arranged that they would put a couple of bags of range balls next to a tree by the tee box at close. Nobody got to work until 5:45 a.m., and I wanted to be practicing already. I put my headphones in and went through a specific routine for ninety minutes and then was off to the short game area to practice for an hour. In the evening I would come out after work, go through a quick warm-up, and play as many holes as I could get in. The owners of the course let me play for free because they knew what I was trying to accomplish. It was the same routine on the weekends, but instead of going to work at seven thirty a.m., I would set up a game, play eighteen holes, go back to the practice range afterward, and work on a few things before going home midafternoon.

Going all in was magical for me. Everyone knew what I was trying to do. Everyone supported me deeply in my quest because they saw how hard I was working. I wanted it so bad I could taste it. The day of the qualifier I was quite nervous. I had played competitive golf since I was thirteen years old. The difference was, I had never gone all in, never announced a clear goal to my loved ones, never practiced as hard as possible. On this day, my dad caddied for me—I always played remarkably well when my dad came to walk with me during matches. I have countless examples of this. It was almost spooky. He calmed me and gave me exceptional confidence.

My nerves were on fire until I striped my first tee ball down the middle. I played quite well considering the pressure I had put myself under. I shot 76. For many that probably doesn't sound particularly good, but competitive golf is a different animal, and unless you have been out there trying to make a par on the last two holes because you are pretty confident the cut line is going to be +4 and you are +4 on the seventeenth-hole tee box, you won't understand. It is a totally different game than drinking a few beers with your buddies on a Saturday afternoon.

Remarkably, 76 was good enough to get me into a thir-teen-man playoff for seven spots. I played well enough to work it down to two of us playing for one spot after three playoff holes. We ended up playing nine more holes at even par, and I won on the thirteenth playoff hole with a par. I had qualified. It worked. I went all in and I gave myself the confidence to play well enough to accomplish my goal. If you aren't all in, if you are thinking about plan B instead of staying completely focused on your task at hand, whether it is selling cups of coffee or qual-ifying for a golf tournament, it won't work. Nobody has ever *kind of* tried and produced an amazing result.

Heeding too much advice

The moment you tell people you're starting a business, the unsolicited advice comes pouring in. You know the kind. It usually starts like this:

"You know what you oughta do?"

"Just make sure you don't . . ."

"If there's one thing you have to make sure you do . . ."

Ignore it all. Your new business becomes the easy thing to create small talk, like the weather. People are fascinated by those of us who are willing to lay it all on the line and go for it. Everyone has their two cents to offer, and most of it isn't even worth that.

You have your chosen advisors. If you haven't already done this, let me give you a little tool I have used hundreds of times over the years. Put your circle of advisors together on paper, anywhere from three to six people. When you are facing an issue that is causing you anxiety, put your board together. Not literally but in your mind, imagine sitting around a table with your key advisors. Pose your question and then listen. You know what each of them will say, and they are available whenever and wherever. This isn't the answer for everything, but day to day it can be helpful. Listen to them and them only. This circle will vary over time, but your key people are key for a reason. Nobody will be in that group who you don't know well, and that is what makes it work. You know what they are going to say in 90 percent of the conversation. Now all you have to do is listen.

Another tactic I lived by early in the development of my business was to pretend my mother was always sitting on my left shoulder and my business partner was sitting on my right shoulder. Would they both approve of everything I was doing? Would they be proud of me each and every day when I laid down to go to bed? There were a few questionable nights after hanging out with my hockey buddies, but I am pretty sure my mom understood, and I know my partner was giving me the proverbial high five. This was such a powerful tool for me when I was young and compelled to sloth away an afternoon or have one too many drinks.

Please allow me to go way off in the weeds and touch on something many will find controversial and crazy. I think some of the worst advisors you can depend on in developing your

business are your lawyer and accountant. They are very good
for certain things, and those things are important, but they
know next to nothing about developing a business. They were
good students, they got into good schools, and they are really
good at following the rules. If there is one thing I know about
successful entrepreneurs, it is that most were poor students
and they break rules as sure as my dog will jump up on you if
you walk into my house.

Let me be clear, good lawyers and accountants are critical in
business. I value my relationships in those categories as much
as any relationships I have in my business. I am simply saying
lawyers and accountants aren't as valuable in start-up. Start-up is
a race to get to positive cash flow. You have to generate revenue,
and oftentimes lawyers and accountants give you things to worry
about that get in your way. In start-up, you will no doubt make
mistakes, and the lawyers and accountants will be around to
clean them up for you and that is why they get paid the big bucks.

The problem is that lawyers and accountants are authority
figures, and what they say is given great weight. Use them for
their area of expertise, and ignore everything else. If I had listened to their advice at the beginning, it would have just gotten in
the way. An accountant once said to my business partner and me,
"You're going too fast. You're outpacing yourself." Our response
was, "We need more cash, and slowing down isn't going to get
us more cash." So we fired him. Lawyers and accountants breed
fear, and fear will kill you. You can't be scared; you must blow
forward with extreme confidence.

If you have an attorney who gets hung up on, say, a clause
in a lease, she's just doing her job, which is to protect you from

liability and financial ruin. But if you need to grow your business and open another location fast, heeding this advice will grind your momentum to a halt. A lawyer's job is to point out the risk, but your job is to assess it and decide. Taking risks is what entrepreneurs do.

I wouldn't say I have a blanket ban on advice from these professionals, but the point I'm trying to stress is that they aren't always right, not by a long shot. Sometimes in order to take your business to the next level, you have to do things that are counterintuitive to standard practices. These professionals are steeped in standard practices; that's their job. If you have to take some risks, their advice is helpful to a point. Then you're on your own.

Remember those bankers I told you about in Toledo who put us in default and wanted to liquidate our business? That was the best thing that ever happened to us. In this case, and I would say in many cases, not knowing the potential negative impact freed us up to charge forward. After we got through that incredibly difficult period, I came away with a much more nuanced understanding of how bankers work and the power they have. I understood finance better by seeing what they were focusing on and what metrics were important to them. I also learned that there's no such thing as "relationship banking." In the end, when you are in a moment of great need, when you need the relationship most, it is all about the numbers, and in most circumstances the person you have the relationship with is gone.

Had I been too risk averse, I wouldn't have borrowed the money, and therefore I wouldn't have learned some of the most valuable lessons of my business career. It is the near misses, the almost failures that teach you your most valuable lessons. I know you have heard this a hundred times, but I am here to tell you again. It is true.

Had we taken all the advice of our accountant, our lawyer, and our banker, we would never have almost failed. Also, had we been checking in with our lawyers and accountants constantly and getting their advice, it would have slowed us down remarkably. We almost failed because of our naiveté regarding loan agreements. Had I understood the documents, I might not have done the deal. The deal propelled us forward aggressively and, yes, almost killed us, but we made it through. Had we not done the deal, we certainly wouldn't have the company we have today.

CONCLUSION

This chapter is truthfully the entire premise of this book. I wanted to name the book *Sell More Shit*. My "professionals" told me it wouldn't work well. It would offend people and might come across as a sales book as opposed to a book on start-ups and entrepreneurialism. I promise there is one answer to any problem you have in your start-up: sell more product. It works every time.

When Calvin Klein's business partner Barry Schwartz was asked how much planning they did before starting their business, he said, "We just sold as many coats as we could."[3]

Every successful business learned how to sell a ton of product early on. That's it, take it to the bank: if you want to know how to be successful in your start-up, spend 80 percent of your

---

3   Amar V. Bhide, *The Origin and Evolution of New Businesses* (Oxford University Press, 2003).

energy trying to figure out how to sell more of your core product tomorrow than you did today. My business partner and I have been waking up every morning for twenty years trying to figure out how to sell one more cup of coffee today than we did yesterday. We now sell over sixty thousand per day, and we are just getting started. It is an obsession for us. If selling isn't your obsession, pack your bags, leave your money in the money market account, and take a nice vacation, because business start-up is going to be difficult for you.

Chapter 3

A CAR THAT CAN FLY!

IT WAS SUMMER OF 2009. The economy was dormant, business was marginal, and everyone was crying into their beer. Prosperity was as anachronistic as leaded gasoline, the flip phone, or printed photographs. It sounded something like this:

> "People are holed up. The streets feel empty. How am I supposed to make a living with no traffic?"

> "Went to three banks with full collateral and a solid plan and was told no for three different reasons."

> "People are so scared. Do you think we will ever get back to the way it was? This sucks."

The world was officially in the fetal position. Our company had slowed down. We were still growing—but barely. The mind-set was defeatist, as if there were nothing we could do about our situation. We were all rolled up inside the blanket of negativity, as if we had no say in how we performed. One evening, I had a metaphysical firework show in my heart and soul—the epiphany to end all epiphanies. I was driving home and thinking about a conversation I'd had earlier in the day with a coworker. We were accepting this new reality—everyone else's reality—and we were making it our own. I remember the epiphany emerging as I thought, *If we could build a car that could fly with a price tag of $25,000, we would sell millions and millions of them.* It wouldn't matter what was happening in the economy. It would be something people had never seen before. It would capture people's imaginations. It would add enormous utility to people's lives. Imagine being the first person on the block to own a car that could fly. Millions and millions, period.

It was a little after eight p.m. when I called my business partner and went off the handle. After about two minutes of my rant, Bob interrupted me and said, "Why don't you come over?" When I got there, he poured a couple of heavy scotches, and we started talking. We ended up talking until after midnight in his living room. We needed to make a change. We needed to develop our car that could fly—a business that people could get into for under $200,000, that sold a product everyone wanted to buy, and that was comparably easy to run in the restaurant industry.

It was simple: pre-epiphany, we were opening coffee shops

that cost $320,000 to $350,000. The epiphany didn't come out of the blue, though. My partner and I had been wondering out loud for a few months about our inflated investment. It was a conversation with Fred DeLuca, the founder of Subway, that ended up being the catalyst for change. Much of the following story is paraphrased from my memory. I am quite comfortable the essence of what was being said is accurate, but I can't be certain the words are exact to the conversation from years past.

Bob and I were sitting with him, and he looked me dead in the eye and asked, "Mike, what is your job as the manager of a franchise business?"

I, of course, went through all the traditional roles and responsibilities as I knew them. He sat there with a knowing grin on his face.

He understood the journey he was about to launch for me and my partner. He replied, "Yes, of course you have to do all those things, but your responsibility is to be a steward of your franchisees' capital." He told me our investment was too high. The threshold of positive cash flow had increased to the point where the business was at risk.

He then took the time to explain the concept of incrementalism. A franchise is akin to an oligarchy. There are many people who have great influence. Owners, like us, have (and should have) great sway over the concept and what we do with it. The problem is that there are a thousand good ideas out there, and they only cost a few dollars each to implement. Those dollars add up quickly, and the next thing we knew we were opening coffee shops for $350K, which is a big hurdle when you are trying to make cash flow with a four-dollar cup of coffee.[1]

Fred DeLuca demanded that we lead, to make the hard decisions, and in doing so to make our franchise concept a safe and productive place for our franchise owners' capital. Simply put, our product, the retail coffee shop, wasn't good enough for the marketplace to embrace it, and our growth was slowing. If what you do is comparable to having a car that can fly for $25K, who cares about the economy? Put people into a highly productive business for under $200K, and the market will support it.

How did we do it? We reorganized the team and repurposed the people working in that department. I brought in a general contractor on our payroll. The contractor and I hired an architect whom he had worked with and had a great relationship with for many years. These guys were pros. The mandate we agreed on was to open the most efficient coffee shop in the world for under $200,000. We started with a blank piece of paper, and we started designing. We cut everything out that wasn't core to our business. The only caveat was that the customer wouldn't be able to tell the difference between the old and the new version when they walked in the door.

First, we stopped using solid surfaces and stainless steel for our counters. We eliminated a grab-and-go refrigerator that had a curved glass window, like something you would see at a bakery.

---

1   This included all pre-opening expenses, including signage, training expenses, working capital for ongoing operations after they were open, the initial franchise fee paid to my company, etc. For exact information on the investment in our franchise, please refer to our Franchise Disclosure Document.

We stopped building offices and put desks in the back corner in the back of the house. We eliminated soft seating. We switched from tile in the back of house and bathrooms to vinyl. We got a much better handle on the mechanicals and understood exactly what our stores needed so our operators weren't oversold. We reduced working capital from $40,000 to $30,000, and then we reduced our initial franchise fee by $15,000. In the end, we were able to get the cost down to $220,000 on average, including working capital. If you remove the working capital, we were below $200,000. We did it.

The core product in my business is the franchise store. In 2009, I needed to get people to invest in developing coffee shops. Our investment was inflated, and positive cash flow was a hurdle that seemed to be getting higher and higher. We knew it, and we made a change. Within a year, I was building coffee shops that cost under $220K to open, and five years later, we had so many stores under contract that we temporarily suspended franchising. It worked. It worked because we wouldn't accept what the world gave us. We needed to do something different and better. We figured out what that was and did it, and the change propelled us forward.

During your start-up, you must figure out your car that can fly—and quickly! This is critical because I have watched many people in start-ups stick to their guns with their core product and miss the opportunities the customer was providing. Typically, in a successful business there were a few moments during start-up when the founder made some hard decisions regarding the offering/concept that changed the course of the business and spurred revenue and growth. For Fred DeLuca it was to franchise his concept, which was new at the time; for Ray Kroc at McDonald's it was controlling the real estate for all of his stores, which gave him control of the brand; for Mike Ilitch at Little Caesars it was to not deliver; for Ted Turner it was twenty-four-hour news at CNN; for Mark Zuckerberg it was making picture-sharing a core feature of Facebook. You have to understand what your consumer wants from you and then do it better than anyone else.

You think you know before you open. Rarely is it that simple. Typically, you have to get your product in the hands of the customers and let them play with it, touch it, and smell it (and in my case, operate it), and find out what is working for them and what isn't.

Does your business clearly represent the purpose of that core product? Once it does, you will develop your rallying cry from this purpose; from my experience, it will jump out and scream at you. The rallying cry is critical because it is how customers will define your business and understand what you can do for them. More on this later; first we have to determine your core product. If you try to be all things to all people, you will end up being nothing to everyone. Your mission is to be the best at delivering your core product. Everything else is ancillary.

SELL WHAT PEOPLE ARE BUYING

The good thing is, it doesn't take computational astrophysics to figure out your core product. The simple answer is that it is the stuff people are buying.

When we started our first café, our primary menu board—
the upper left-hand side is what gets the most attention, so
that's where you place your focal products—had all the standard, traditional coffee drinks: lattes, espresso, cappuccino,
Americano, macchiato, con panna, and the like. We then had
a separate menu board next to it with all of our flavored lattes.
It didn't take long to see that most people were buying the flavored lattes. Our data from the point-of-sale system was catego-
rized into four categories: traditions (cappuccinos, espressos,
espressos con panna, macchiatos, Americanos), sweet and
creamy (flavored lattes), food, and merchandise. It became
obvious quickly that the sweet and creamy category was outper-
forming traditions by a factor of three to one. So we flopped the
boards. The board on the left became full of what we call Sweet
Bomb Lattes—caramel, caramel and hazelnut, chocolate and
marshmallow, white and dark chocolate. The next board over
was traditions.

Remember, this was in the 1990s. This focus on sweet
drinks was not a conventional decision among the high-end
coffee enthusiasts and cafés that were just starting to grow in
number. They considered adding two ounces of caramel to a
latte a violation of epicurean manners, as if we were pouring
melted cheese on a lobster tail. Most of our competition were
traditionalists, sticking to their rigid coffee ideology, most likely
at the expense of revenue and their bottom line. If we had
identified as a traditional Italian espresso bar, we most likely
wouldn't have made this shift; we would have stuck to promoting traditional drinks. We had to shift our identity to something

like the ice cream store for adults and start selling Sweet Bomb Lattes. We started marketing the gooey, whipped-cream-covered drinks, and we are here to tell about it twenty years later, with one of the most successful retail coffee brands in America.

When I talk to people about why their businesses don't work, rarely does someone say, "I just haven't figured out what will sell and how to sell it." Instead, it's always external factors beyond their control—excuses.

When you own a start-up business, you have one person to blame if you can't achieve revenue and therefore cash flow. If you aren't smart enough to figure out what the consumer wants to buy from you—what your core product is—and start banging product out the door, you'll fail. Your business isn't failing; *you* are! It's not the economy's fault. It's not the weather. It's not the competition. It's your fault. You have to laser in on your product, understand it and why the customer wants to buy it, and then sell it.

One of the great examples of people who understand their business and why people buy their stuff is Mark Zuckerberg of Facebook. He noticed that the members were changing out their profile pictures regularly. If you remember, early on at Facebook, it wasn't simple and easy for the customer to change their profile picture. Zuckerberg quickly realized that photos were the core of why people were using the site: people wanted to share their lives in pictures with their friends and family. Facebook worked hard to make it simple for people to share pictures, and people embraced the site. Mark Zuckerberg credits that realization as one of the key moments in the development of his successful start-up. Simply said, he was paying attention to how the customer was using the site, and he facilitated that use. He could have easily missed that the core product was pictures if he had been stuck thinking of Facebook as a directory.[2]

A friend of mine, a software developer, was starting a company about fifteen years ago. He was writing code to streamline the manufacturing process in large factories. As he was going around selling to prospective customers, he was learning what they wanted, what would make their jobs easier. He kept hearing over and over again about how they needed a secure place to store all their information. They weren't buying much of his software; it turns out they didn't need a marginally developed piece of software that solved a problem they didn't know they had. They needed data storage.

There's no way he could have had any idea that this need existed if he hadn't made those six calls a day for months and years on end. But that was only part of it. The crucial thing was what he did with this information: he altered his business. To be sure, writing groundbreaking software is much more glamorous than data storage. Yet there was a clearly defined need for data storage, so he started storing data. A lot of people would have missed this opportunity and stayed the course selling their baby, their passion—in his case, the software. Many people early in the coffee business wanted to keep trying to sell traditional Italian-style drinks such as cappuccinos, macchiatos, con pannas, and lattes. This was their idea of the business. But

---

2   "Mark Zuckerberg at Startup School 2012," YouTube, published October 25, 2013, https://www.youtube.com/watch?v=5bJi7k-y1Lo.

the American consumer wasn't ready; the American consumer wanted Sweet Bomb Lattes.

Fast-forward fifteen years, and my friend hasn't written a new piece of software in a decade, but he's got a seven-figure income. Data storage exploded as an industry over that time. It's not a stretch to say that most aspiring entrepreneurs who write code for a living would enjoy the business my friend has today. He decided to switch his entire direction based on what the customers told him they wanted. Data storage wasn't sexy, but there sure was a need.

BIGGBY could have easily overlooked that people were buying Sweet Bomb Lattes. Mark Zuckerberg could have easily dismissed the volume of pictures being swapped out daily. My friend could have missed the growing market for data storage. You must be in touch with your customers. Let them tell you about your "car that can fly."

This sounds simple: let your customers tell you what they want by paying attention to both their behavior and their purchases. But this part can be harder than you imagine. Let me paint a picture for you. In our original cafés, we had a well-developed food menu. It was fairly typical for that time. We had soups, salads, and sandwiches. Our food was good but not outstanding, and it was expensive. We didn't have the buying power to compete with the food concepts on price, and to make things worse, their product was better than ours. In order to understand the dynamic, we had to put our ego in our pocket. People were coming into our stores with food from other restaurants, sitting down with a coffee, and eating. They would walk in with a Subway sandwich or even a breakfast sandwich from a competitor. Our visceral reaction was to focus on how rude it was to walk into our cafés with outside food. "How could they think that is OK?" It took some real awareness to understand that they were complimenting us: they loved our drinks! They loved our drinks enough to stop somewhere else to get food and then come to get their favorite drink from our store. The food they were bringing into our store was a better value, but they couldn't go anywhere else to get a drink as delicious as ours. So, instead of asking them not to bring in outside food, we embraced it. We eventually got out of the lunch business and focused on our core product.

This goes for verbal feedback as well. Typically, your customers won't tell you what they don't like. They just adapt or they go away. When a customer is willing to tell you what they don't like about your product, you have to treat that feedback like gold. It is hard to hear. Many managers of the business in start-up gloss over the root cause of the feedback; they don't dive deep and actually listen. They simply try to appease the customer and make the customer happy. The important part in that moment is to make sure you are listening and recording their commentary. It is so easy to cop an attitude based on the drama of the moment and completely miss the message. An example: from the beginning we have been told our products are great and our people are amazing, but the experience is a little too expensive. This is hard to hear. They are right! We are constantly paying attention to this, and we are addressing it through an aggressive rewards program and through discounting. People love coming into our stores and buying our products. We have to make sure they are feeling like they are getting value. We could lower our price across the board, but a large segment of people enjoy our product and are willing to pay full price. For them there is plenty of value. For those who believe our product is a little pricey, we work hard to identify them and provide them a discount. Who needs a discount, who doesn't, how often they need it, and for how much—this nuance is a pivotal part of our business. We understand that, and we work hard every day to figure it out.

You have to put your ego in your pocket and pay attention. Pay attention to the customer's behavior and what they are buying. Most certainly, pay attention to what they are telling you. This seems so obvious that it's silly, but I am here to tell you, I see businesspeople who are so wrapped up in their own ego-infused fog that they don't have the ability to understand exactly what the customer is saying. Listen closely and carefully; it will help you refine and improve your offering so the customer will want to buy more product from you.

But figuring it out is only the first step. Next, you have to execute.

GOOD WON'T GET IT DONE

Once you have figured out what people want to buy, you had better be damn good at providing it. You'd better be the best. If you don't deliver on your promise, a first-time customer will never come back. Your product must be perfect. Period.

Some—very few—businesses achieve success simply by securing the perfect location, being first to a market, or having some irrational advantage over their competition. For example, you open an ice cream shop on the beach of a busy resort town, and you'll do bang-on business three months of the year. It probably doesn't matter how good your product is; people are going to buy from you. But for most of us, product quality is mission critical.

As we saw in chapter 1, the percentage of start-ups that will be around and thriving after ten years is very low. It's as if you're in school and only the top-performing students (straight As) in the class pass the course. In business, you have to be in that top tier of a class full of really hardworking, smart people who are ambitious enough to start their own company. More simply stated, you have to be in the top tier of a subset of people who are extremely capable and hell-bent on succeeding. In this group, if you do B+ work, you will fail. It is daunting to say the least.

As trite as it may sound, part of earning an A+ is believing in the importance of earning the highest grade. Why does it need to be your obsession? For example, you only have one opportunity to make a great first impression, and it is almost impossible to make a great first impression with a merely good product. When your business is brand new, you are always making first impressions—every hour of every day. People are coming to your website, either reaching out to you after googling your service and clicking your link or being funneled to your website through some electronic advertising you have done. The most difficult thing in a start-up business is convincing someone to engage your business; once they do, you have to capitalize on that opportunity with a perfect product. A strong first impression allows you to start building a long-term relationship with that customer.

If the first impression is mediocre, that opportunity—and that long-term relationship—is compromised.

Example A: I have been a low-single-digit handicap golfer for most of my life. I have been off the rails for about five years now with my newly formed blended family and a two-year-old baby boy monopolizing my wife and me. Just this summer I have been able to find time to re-engage. I am playing a ton better and feeling good about my game again. I was listening to the PGA Tour radio a couple of weeks ago, and they were interviewing a golf pro who had developed an application for smartphones that would help you track your data. When you finish each hole, you go in and click four or five buttons, and the app kicks out your core data at the end of a round and accumulates it over time. Good players record, track, and use data to help them get better. It has always been cumbersome, but not now! Somebody has solved my problem. I was so excited I downloaded the app while driving (sorry, Mom), and as soon as I got to work, I logged in. But then my password didn't work. I tried three different times to figure out the log-in process, and I couldn't make it work. Once I was able to log in, I tried to play a phantom round to see how it worked. It was really difficult, and I stopped after five minutes. I was disappointed. I wanted this product in my life, and the execution of my first experience let me down. I most likely won't go back.

Example B: There is a new speakeasy-type bar here in Ann Arbor, the kind of place that has no sign out front. You walk in the door and it almost feels like they don't want you there. There is a gorgeous hipster mostly ignoring you, and you feel like you are interrupting something important to ask for a table. This all works; this is their vibe, I understand. My wife and I, along with another couple, get seated, and we wait, forever. Finally, another breed of hipster approaches our table to take our order. He is quite knowledgeable, and we engage and place our orders. We are just coming off a dining experience where salt was the main ingredient. My wife asks for waters all around. We wait, we wait, and we wait. Finally, our drinks, made by the "mixologist," are delivered. My wife wonders out loud about our waters. There is no way any of us are going to be able to enjoy our bourbon concoctions without a side of water. Our water never arrives. The drinks might have been perfectly prepared, but because of a small nuance in product, a glass of water, we ended up leaving after one drink to go to our standard watering hole to finish the night. We were totally interested in this place. We were excited to go and explore the new option in our town. The product experience was marginal due to a lack of execution. Game over.

As for me, I am in the franchise business. People inquire every single day about franchising. For many years, I laid down the mandate that when a potential franchisee inquired via our website, I wanted someone to make a phone call within one minute. I even flirted with staffing the site 24/7, but people in my organization talked me out of it. The word *overkill* was mentioned. I was called obsessive. But that's the point. My product, as a franchise company, is the store itself and getting people to sign up to build a store of their own. We support owner-operators in building great businesses. If a prospective owner-operator calls, I want them to be overwhelmed by the level of our engagement. I want them to feel our excitement and enthusiasm related to their inquiry. I want them to feel an overwhelming amount of support from the first time they contact our company.

There was a time when I was involved in calling the leads myself. I specifically remember a lead that came in, and I called the guy back within thirty seconds. He picked up the phone, I introduced myself, and he chuckled. "Boy," he said, "you were quick about that. I just hit send a second ago!"

My reply was, "There is a lot of coffee flowing around our office, so we can be a touch excitable. I am really glad you inquired into our company. Let's get started: What would be helpful for you?"

In my soul I know this made a strong first impression.

In your new business, you had better be ready to provide the A+ level product. You have to be focused on being the very best. Your business will grow aggressively if your customers fall in love with you and your product, but they'll never fall in love with a B+. In start-up, that first engagement is mission critical. Your goal should be that your people and even your customers are calling you obsessive, a control freak, a perfectionist. If they are, I think you are on the right track.

THE CAR WILL NOT FLY ON ITS OWN

The father of a good friend of mine was a pilot. He flew primarily small, private planes for the wealthy. He was a wonderful storyteller with a mind full of tales. One Friday night, at his favorite Mexican restaurant and after a few margaritas, we were talking about air safety. He asked me, "Mikey, do you know why planes crash? Because when something goes wrong, the pilot forgets to fly the plane."

Flying the plane—or flying that car from earlier in the chapter—is a twofold proposition. There is the mechanical component, meaning the plane has to be maintained and function properly. Theoretically, it will get off the ground and fly in the direction you desire and then land where you want it to land. Generally, I think the mechanical part of flying is the easiest for the pilot. You need to make sure you have the right maintenance program in place, and before you take off you need to work the checklist to make sure everything is tip-top.

The analogy between flying a plane and the development and execution of your business is apt. The mechanical components of flying your plane or developing your business are important. It is defining your core product and all of the policies and procedures that make your business run. It is writing the schedule. It is the quality control methods. It is the maintenance programs on all of your equipment. This is the stuff that has to be happening for the business to work. This is the easy stuff. Let me say that again: *this is the easy stuff.* You wake up in the morning, review your checklist, do your tasks, and feel accomplished.

Additionally—and I hope I can make this point clear—there is a misstep people can make in developing their businesses. You have to control where the plane goes, how fast, at what elevation, and in what direction. All of this is controlled by your hands on the joystick. The mechanics are irrelevant if you are not directing every move. Your job as the pilot of your business is to make sure you are communicating your message, pulling the levers necessary for people to become aware of your business. As the pilot of your business, you must make sure you are tweaking, twisting, pulling the right levers, and turning the right knobs to ensure you are promoting your product, communicating your message so there is a reason for people to think about your business and hopefully give you a try. And that's all you are looking for: that they give you a try. Once you have been able to maneuver your joystick perfectly and get them to consider you, the mechanics will then have a chance to work. If you aren't flying your business properly, the mechanics never get a chance to work.

I find many people forget about flying the plane and spend most of their time worrying about the mechanics. Maneuvering your business through the complicated marketplace in a way that garners attention and generates revenue is extremely difficult. I have noticed many times over that when a business isn't working perfectly—and they never do—the owner spends an enormous amount of time on the mechanics and completely loses focus on flying the plane quickly and on the correct course. Fly the plane. It can still work with mechanical issues. It can't work if nobody is at the joystick. Without a pilot, it will crash every time; mechanical issues rarely bring a plane down on their own.

So what do you do with your hands on the joystick? Once you figure out what you do best, once you have figured out your core product and are committed to aggressively flying the plane, it's time to start telling people over and over again. You are never done explaining to anyone who will listen what your product is and why it is better. You have to scream it at your customer at every opportunity. This takes patience and persistence. If you think you're being aggressive with your messaging, I guarantee you it's not enough.

WRITE A TAGLINE THAT FITS ON A BUMPER STICKER

Now you have to develop the bumper sticker you will proudly put on your flying car. As you are flying your car around, you want to tell everyone about it. People won't take the time to read three paragraphs on your business; you need to communicate what the heck you are selling—what value you can bring them—in under three seconds. Pique their interest. Get them to think, *Huh, that sounds interesting.* Boom. You have them. There is a chance that they will look into your company in more detail or give your product a try.

I think most people consider taglines to be part of marketing or advertising. I don't. I consider them to be part of your product. The tagline, the three to five words you use to describe the value you are bringing to the customer, is as critical as the widget you build or the service you provide. It may be slightly unconventional to put the tagline in the chapter on product, but getting people's attention in relation to a product is as important as the product itself. For example, the tagline for a flying car could be "elevate above," the tagline for this book "sell more shit." The BIGGBY tagline for awhile was "hip sip in a zip." Three to five words that express the value you bring and who you are.

At BIGGBY, our message is about those Sweet Bomb Lattes. Rarely do we do something that's off this message. We are going to sell you a latte with some kind of syrup in it with whipped cream on top. It took years of remarkable consistency, but that's what we're known for now. We are currently transitioning to a new tagline that will have more to do with love and awareness.

One key is to simplify your message. I go through my inbox every morning, and I delete, delete, delete. At times, I will take a moment and think back about which emails engaged my attention, and it's always the ones that have a clear message. In 98 percent of professional emails, you have to figure out what they're offering. The message is convoluted. It takes time to decipher what they are trying to sell you. Get to the point and quickly. If I am interested in what you are offering, I will click through or I will visit. You have my attention for a split second. If you can't grab my attention, I am gone.

Building a clear message is as important as building the perfect product. This sounds simple, but it's amazing how many times I ask business owners, "What is your core product? What does your business do?" and they don't know what to say. If they don't have the answer ready to go, they've lost me. I don't have time to listen to you explain your business for five minutes, and neither does anyone else. It's about clarity, consistency, and repetition.

The best example of a clear message in the past two decades has been the Jimmy John's "Freaky Fast" campaign. They latched onto and sent the message over and over until almost anyone would say "freaky fast" if you mentioned Jimmy John's. What is your freaky fast message? Does it fit on a bumper sticker that can be read and understood if your car goes flying by somebody at thirty-five miles per hour?

Some of my other favorite campaign slogans include "Just do it," "Got milk?," "Can you hear me now?," "I'm lovin' it," "A diamond is forever," "The quicker picker upper," and "Finger-lickin' good."

Though BIGGBY used the tagline "Hip sip in a zip" early on in our development, we walked away from it because we didn't think it matched up with who we are. We aren't really hip, and we didn't think saying we were hip and then not delivering on that message was going to work. But when we laid it to rest, we didn't have a message anymore. It hurt our business. We spent a number of years searching for our next message. People understand repetition and consistency. They like to know what you are doing for them in a three-second sound bite. Be clear and concise; it's the clarity piece—pardon the pun—that's more opaque.

Once you think you have a clear and focused message and you're ready to try it, turn to your inner circle for feedback. After you've been working your message over and over again, throwing stuff out and then picking it back out of the trash again, you're in no position to be able to judge with any accuracy how effective it is. Ask the people you trust, and make sure they're able to be critical. An interviewing tip is to make sure you ask the inner circle straightforward, open-ended questions: What does this say to you? What do you think of the colors/font? What's missing? Let them say what images, feelings, and ideas come to mind, and just listen. Do not ask yes or no questions like, "Do you like the color orange here?"

It's worth noting that this process doesn't get any better after the start-up phase. You must always be refining and focusing your message. We spend a fortune on branding at BIGGBY, and there are still people in the state of Michigan—a lot of people—who don't know who we are, and they don't care. This is after twenty years of our big orange signs multiplying everywhere. That's our fault. We need to be finding new and different ways every week, every month, every quarter to be introducing our brand to new people. We need to be getting new and different people reading our tagline. Maybe this summer we sponsor a hot air balloon with the tagline on the side. Maybe next fall we take a page out of the Mail Pouch chewing tobacco company's book and paint our tagline on the side of five hundred barns throughout the state of Michigan. Maybe we sponsor every AA and Al-Anon meeting with our tagline on every cup served. Everyone gets complacent. In start-up, when you are struggling to get to your first day of cash flow, you have to be aggressively engaged and make sure you are constantly thinking of new and interesting ways to get your brand noticed. What does getting your brand noticed mean? It isn't impressions (to me, brand impressions are not powerful); it means getting someone to see your brand, read your tagline, and think, *Huh, that sounds interesting.*

DROP YOUR LEAFLETS BY THE BUSHEL LOAD

Now that you have your message, we have to load up the trunk of your flying car and start dropping your message on everyone, everywhere, all of the time. Give everyone you know one hundred pamphlets, and ask them to give them away. Get five thousand stickers produced, and start putting them on everything and anything. I see promotional stickers stuck on street signs or lampposts, on mail boxes, on windows—and I love it. One of our great initiatives when we are promoting a new store in a new market is to go into a superstore parking lot and put flyers and coupons under the windshield wipers of every car in the lot. In the end, the customer has to reach up and pull our pamphlet off their windshield before driving away, and more often than not, they are going to read our tagline. Is this aggressive? You bet. Does it work? Absolutely. If you believe in your product and your tagline communicates your value, then get out there and promote it (side note: expect to get kicked out of parking lots).

It is surprising to me how many business managers are shy about promoting their businesses. If you believe you are bringing value to the consumer and your product is something that will improve their lives, why wouldn't you want to tell everyone you meet? If your product brings as much value as a car that can fly for $25,000, then people are going to thank you for telling them about it. If you don't believe enough to slap a sticker on a fence post or slide 145 pamphlets under windshield wipers, then you need to take a second to reflect on whether you have the chops to be in business. Remember, this is a start-up. You are in the fight of your life. Later you won't have to be this aggressive, but during start-up it is critical to put the pedal down, grab the wheel, and fly your car as fast and aggressively as you can. If you do, you might just have a chance.

Chapter 4

THE BEST ADVERTISING MONEY CAN'T BUY

ADVERTISING DURING START-UP IS like concessions for a sports team. Your audience expects you to have it (you need radio or banner ads like a baseball team needs to sell hot dogs), but it doesn't make you play—or sell—any better.

So here's what you do: focus on a few key ad buys in your local market. Where do you learn about businesses like yours—TV ads during the local news, print ads in your community newsletter, targeted ads on an all-powerful search engine, radio ads during morning drive time, social media ads/promotions, banner ads on certain domains? If the space is affordable, buy a small ad there. If it's too pricey, find something else, but don't overthink it. You need to get your name out there a bit, but advertising is always a gamble, so don't wager your rent when you can spend that energy and capital on your product.

In a start-up, for most budgets your traditional marketing and advertising spend (as opposed to your guerrilla marketing effort) is inconsequential. You simply don't have the resources to move the needle in the real world. Keep it simple and affordable: choose a couple of small advertising moves, put them in place for a year, and don't think about them again for eleven months. Now, get back to promoting your business.

My partner and I do a ton of speaking in front of prospective owner-operators/franchisees, and at one point in our standard presentation, my partner asks, "What is the number one way to generate more customers to your new business?" Invariably, the answer is marketing and advertising. He is then quick to say, "Nope, advertising and marketing only work when there is a product and experience behind the brand that people fall in love with. First you must have the product and experience, and then advertising complements your efforts."

Most importantly, you need to focus on your customer and your product. As we discussed in the previous chapters, your goal is to sell the best cup of coffee (or whatever your product or service is) you can and keep your customers coming back. Treat your customers like they are everything, give them a product they love, and you'll have the best advertising money can't buy: word of mouth.

YOUR FIRST CRUSH

Remember how you felt about your first crush—the first time you looked at someone and thought, *I would do anything for this person.* That puppy love took 100 percent of your attention when they were in the room and 85 percent when they weren't. You noticed their every move, and your mood changed to match, focused on each of their changes of facial expression. You had crazy, effervescent energy pumping through your veins. You felt alive for the first time in your life. Now you understood why all the love stories were so powerful, what everyone had been talking about.

Your customers need to be a first crush for your business. They should be everything to you. You must read into every raised eyebrow and live and die by their every breath. Just like your first crush, you must be willing to do anything for them, to make sure they notice and are impressed by you.

There's one big difference, though. When you are a kid in love, the outcome doesn't really matter (although it sure feels like it). If you get rejected, you move on. We have all lived through it and come out the other side. It was difficult, but we'd love and laugh again soon enough. But for a start-up, getting the customer to fall in love with you is ten times more important than your first crush. The future of your business depends on it. Your future depends on it.

When you get your customer to fall in love with you—with your product, your service, your app, your shop—they'll tell their friends about you. They'll rave to their parents about how well you treat them. They'll invite colleagues for a cup of coffee with you. They'll spread the word, creating more customers to fall in love with you. You have to cultivate that first relationship so you can start cultivating each new one, which will each branch out to new ones. This is how you exponentially grow your business!

DROP THAT ZERO, AND GET WITH A HERO

However, in business it is often much harder than it was as a teenager to woo that special someone. The problem in business is that the customer is surely already "dating" someone else. Do you remember having a crush on someone who already had a boyfriend or girlfriend? It was the worst feeling to see them walking through the hallways holding hands with somebody else. Every time you saw it, you wanted to puke on your shoes.

In business, everyone is holding hands with someone else. They are buying their milk somewhere, they prefer a certain car dealership, they are loyal to another brand of coffee, they have a travel site they book with, and they have been buying the same brand of jeans for twenty-five years. They have their three or four sites online where they spend 90 percent of their digital money. They like (and, dare I say, even love) the people in their daily routine: the cashier at the corner convenience store, the grandma sweeping up hair at the salon, the pimple-faced teenager scooping popcorn at the movie theater, and the manager of the produce section at the grocery store. You and your new start-up are asking them to leave behind that other relationship and spend their precious time and money with you. This is hard, because people like the comfortable, and routine brings comfort. Comfort is a powerful tool, and you have to first undermine it, then make it yours.

When BIGGBY opens a store in a market with little or no competition, we generally thrive. When we open in a market with significant competition, it is much more difficult to build revenue (rocket science, eh?). Where there is competition, the people who are willing to buy gourmet coffee outside of their home already have a routine, and you have to convince them to break that routine. In order to convince them, you have to ping them over and over, you have to compel them to give you a try, and you have to get them to walk in the door.

There is no silver bullet. Surely, there are a million answers to how you get a customer to walk through your door, or engage your app, or call your 1-800 number, or click on your link. That said, there are some fundamentals you need to be following. They have been stated in other places within the book, but restating them here meets one of the fundamentals: repetition. First, what is your powerful, simple message? Write it, make sure you love it, and make sure it is on point and summarizes what you are doing with your business. Now, post it, say it, scream it, write it, or whisper it wherever you can imagine. Repeat: post it, say it, scream it, write it, or whisper it wherever you can imagine. Repeat: post it, say it, scream it, write it, or whisper it wherever you can imagine. Repetition is critically important.

Give away your product for free if that is what it takes. Potential customers may need this to try you and therefore have the opportunity to fall in love. Wooing is the art of getting somebody to pay attention to you long enough to land a message that convinces them to give you a shot. If you have to buy that moment by giving them a free product, so be it. Seize your moment.

We used to fill up huge garbage bags with plastic reusable coffee mugs and throw them over our shoulder like Santa Claus. Inside each mug was a free beverage card and a frequency card stamped nine out of twelve times. We walked into office buildings, entered all of the suites, and handed out ten to fifteen per suite. The potential fanatic would be able to walk in and get a free drink of their choice on visit one; then we would stamp their card and show them they only had to come back two more times to earn a free drink. This program would get them in the door four times. We believed we could birth a fanatic in four visits. We had one owner-operator executing this program who donned an orange cape with the gaudiest, hugest white sunglasses and announced he was Captain Coffee, here to save the day. People loved it. Many, many times he was invited to put a mug on every desk in the office.

Last note: How would you be acting if I was willing to write you a check for $500,000 in three months if we were hitting some threshold of revenue? My guess is that you would be obsessed. Everyone you run into, everyone you talk to, in whatever setting, is somebody you can potentially turn into a fanatic of your business. It doesn't matter if you are in line at the grocery store, walking the dog at a rest area on the freeway, dropping off your milk jugs at the recycling center, or filling up your car at the corner gas station. Every person you see, every one person you have the opportunity to come into contact with, is a golden opportunity to gain a fanatic of your business. Yep, bold is beautiful. Shy doesn't work. It's like with dating: the gregarious, outgoing person is going to go on more dates than the shy person standing in the corner and leaning up against the wall.

My friend David is a beautiful human being. The kind of person your kids fall in love with the first time they meet him. When we were in college, I always loved going out with David, as he would always have a deck of cards and liked to sit down at a table full of girls and ask if they enjoyed magic. Everyone loves magic. Next thing you knew, we would all be hanging out and talking about what a nut job David was, but we were all secretly thankful for David because we had eight new friends. Is it possible for you to sit down at a table full of strangers and strike up a conversation? If not, you have to find a way to make that happen. You woo by starting the conversation.

THEY'VE TAKEN YOUR HAND! NOW WHAT? DANCE, YOU FOOL . . . DANCE!

Getting a new customer to walk in the door is just the beginning. Now you have to impress the hell out of them. Once they have decided to give you a whirl, you have to talk them into going steady with you. You have to become their regular thing. This means you have to be perfect, you have to make an impact, and you have to make them swoon. They have to be blown away by you and your attention.

Example: One of my hockey buddies, a fellow Bomber, is an orthopedic surgeon. Back when he was just getting into his practice, we were playing in a tournament one weekend and had a ton of downtime. I asked him questions about his work— not about surgery or fixing knees, but about the business side of his practice. How did he get new business? I saw billboards with his pretty face on them all over town. What percent of their revenue did they put into advertising? How did leads come in? What did they do after surgery for their customers? Did they have any way of staying in touch with their patients over time?

He said they did spend a lot on advertising but that their business came almost entirely from referrals (that's code for *professional word of mouth*). Typically, the patient's primary care doctor recommended his practice. This made it a bit more complicated, since he had two customers—his patient and their primary care doctor—but the best approach was the same for both of them.

I was shocked to learn the doctor had little if any contact with the patient or the primary care doctor post-surgery. There was little concern about how the patient fared throughout the process and into recovery and beyond. Where was the love? Where was the genuine concern for the patient? We had a long conversation about what an opportunity this offered him to stand out as a surgeon. I recommended the following:

First, he needed to provide top-notch service to his patients. He needed to follow up with them right after surgery to make sure they were healing, and again after thirty days or so to ensure that the surgery had been successful. Then he needed to add them to a mailing list for helpful exercises and recovery tips—if those tips were relevant to the patient (that is, he should offer something they find useful, not pester them). He'd send them a card on their birthday and check back when appropriate to make sure they were happy with the results of their surgery. In other words, he needed to let his patient know they were important and cared for.

Why? So when the primary care doctor asked the patient about their surgical experience, my friend's "customer service" would guarantee that the patient would rave about him to the primary care doc. As this started to happen more often, the primary care doctor's referrals would increase, often exclusively to his practice and specifically to my friend.

Then, he needed to follow up with the primary care doctor, too. He'd make sure that they knew he appreciated each referral, and he'd communicate his surgical consults and the results of surgery clearly and quickly so the physician could communicate efficiently with the patient on their end. With this successful seduction, these doctors would not only start referring more patients, but also begin singing my friend's praises to other doctors, widening his customer base.

Around a year later, my friend and I were sitting together in the locker room, and he brought up our discussion. He said he'd implemented the patient attention and physician service into his practice, with some initial resistance from his own partners. When he started, the other doctors in his practice said he was nuts. His business manager explained how risky it was to engage personally and directly. But he gave it a shot, and the number of referrals skyrocketed. He was getting a staggeringly higher number of new patients and the most amazing reviews in his career from both patients and referring docs.

The stupidly simple thing about this is that he didn't become a better surgeon. He was already a great surgeon performing at a high level. But now he backed up his work with excellent customer attention and care. He began to let his customers know he cared. What is crazy is he did always care and cared deeply. As a doctor, that simple act of empathy and attention made him stand out.

In my life, I have noticed that when people in business try to connect with their customers—when they try really hard—people notice, and they appreciate it. They want to do business with you and support your effort. The customer can smell mediocre, can taste marginal, can sense apathy. If you are only kind of doing your best, it simply won't work. Just like that first crush, you have to romance your customer to catch their eye, then amaze them with attention and care to build a relationship.

ASKING FOR YOUR CUSTOMER'S SUPPORT

And that relationship runs two ways; it's mutual. When you support your customer with a mind-blowing experience, top-notch service, and a quality product, they'll support you with referrals. This is the most powerful marketing engine on the planet: a referral from one friend or family member to another. If my brother tells me about some new restaurant across town where he loved his experience, I am going to give it a try. Without his referral, what is the chance I would end up in that spot for dinner on Friday night across town? Next to zero.

But sometimes, like in a relationship, you don't get what you need. Your customers might take you for granted. Maybe they want to keep their favorite spot to themselves, or maybe they just don't think to spread the word. The only way to make sure they know what you need is to tell them.

You have to ask your customers to promote you. Yes, you have to put your ego in your back pocket, and you have to beg and plead with people to promote your business. If this is hard for you or you feel awkward, get over it. If you are too shy, if you are too reserved and you aren't going to be willing to aggressively promote your business and ask others to do the same, I am afraid your start-up is doomed. If you want a successful business, you have to ask people to help you build it. If there is one way to never get a date, it is to never ask somebody out. It is the same in business. You have to ask; you have to tell people what you want. You have to be clear with them about your intentions and then ask them to help you.

Let me give you a snippet of how this works. A customer has been coming into my store for a few weeks every other day, and I notice they start to come in every day. I am supercharged with them; I know they must be loving the experience with me and my business. The drinks are perfect, I am super quick with production, and I engage them like I am engaging my brother after a victory and a few beers in the locker room. Frankly, I am having a blast, and I am pretty sure they are enjoying me and the experience, too. At some point, I decide I am going to go for it: I am going to ask them to promote me. This is the exchange:

"Frank, you love me, right?"

There is a pause, and Frank smiles, chuckles, and replies, "Sure, Mike. I love you."

I continue, "You love my business, too, right?"

Frank replies, "Yep."

"Here is the deal. I love my business. I love doing this, and I really want my business to be successful. I have designs on turning this into a great company. I want to be the best coffee shop chain in the world.

Would you be willing to promote my business to your friends and family? I promise when they come in and tell me Frank sent them, I will make them feel like royalty. You know I will. What do you say? I would be really grateful."

Frank says, "Yeah, of course I will."

That is it, end of story. That's the end of the conversation, and I never have to bring it up again. Frank leaves and feels good about me and about his experience. I was genuine, open, and honest with him, not trying to be cheap and cheesy. I simply want his help growing my business. He feels good, and I think there is a good chance he will, in his own way and however he feels comfortable, promote me to others.

It all starts with that first question: Do you love me? If you aren't 100 percent certain they are going to answer the question affirmatively, then don't start. You have to have built that relationship already. They have to love you and your business before you start asking for things. But then, once you are certain, all you have to do is ask.

This example might seem quite retail focused. I think dentists can ask their patients point blank to refer them. I think technology companies can reach out directly to customers and build relationships. My "car guy" asked me the other day if I would recommend him to my family and friends. I think no matter the business, it is possible to figure out how to make a connection and ask the customer to promote you. Most everyone is familiar with the Net Promoter Score (NPS) rating. I would like to change it from, "Would you tell somebody about us" and add one more line, "If you rated us a nine or a ten, will you please promote us to three or four people today?" It is more aggressive and clearly demonstrates we are actively interested in growing our business.

I will never forget, in the early days I had a business partner, Mary. She was amazing at aggressively promoting our business. The Michigan Restaurant Association was hosting an event at the local minor league baseball stadium. They invited different restaurant concepts from around the state to come set up booths on the concourse. Lansing being the capital, they invited all the legislators to come to lunch on a Friday and stroll the booths, sampling food and drink. We were invited to assemble a booth. We had just opened a store across the street from the capitol building a few months prior to the event, so the legislators and their staff were a primary target of our potential customer base. Mary was hell-bent on making a good impression.

She quickly realized the guests were being a little reserved and not engaging at our booth, so she grabbed a tray, loaded it up with drinks (some version of a flavored iced latte with whipped cream on top), and went to the entrance of the event. She started handing out drinks. She wasn't asking if they wanted one; she was putting the drinks in their hands as if it was part of the program. It was brilliant! She grabbed somebody else on our staff and started shuttling trays of drinks between our booth and the entrance. I was in the booth making drink after drink as fast as I could, trying to keep up.

Later, as they walked past our booth, she would engage them, "How was your drink? Do you want to try something else? No? OK then, but here is my card. We just opened a shop across from the capitol building. Come and see us! Bring somebody with you. We'll make whatever you want. It was great meeting you!"

We *owned* the event!

Mary was growing the business by asking for what we needed. Her attitude was *We are really good at what we do, we opened the business to make money, and we need a ton of customers, so let's work really hard to get people to come in the door.* That shop across from the capitol took off. We had staffers and legislators caffeinated and ready to govern, and we still do today, over twenty-one years later.

Once the customer is in love, you have to ask them point-blank to promote you to others. At BIGGBY, we have always been great at developing fans, but we are even better at asking them to help us promote and build our business. It is core to what we do and who we are. It is one of the reasons we have been successful at building a franchise concept. We ask others every day to help us build this brand, to get on board this bullet train and promote us like crazy!

There is the big secret. If you want a powerful relationship with your customers, you have to get vulnerable and ask, and if you want your customers to promote you to others, you have to ask them to do that, too. I see so many people who are reserved, almost shy; reserved and shy have no place in the world of start-up.

AUTHENTICITY

The basis of a loving relationship is trust. As the business owner, your trust will be violated, and quite frankly it will hurt, but it is part of the business. To this day, twenty years later, my heart sinks when I see a friend, family member, or loyal customer holding the cup of one of my competitors. I have worked so hard to build my company; I have tried to be good to everyone, and then somebody I care about is thoughtless enough to show up with a cup from the big green death star. It hurts more than you think it would.

You can't always make your customers monogamous—or mono-caféous, in my case. But you can make their experience with you and your business shine in comparison, through honest and positive interactions and better coffee. They might stop by "Charbucks" for a quickie, but they'll always come back for your sweet, sweet latte.

If we agree that our goal should be to have a loving, caring relationship with our customers, then let me share another secret with you: the secret to building a trusting relationship with your customer is authenticity. In today's marketplace, the customer is tired of being lied to. They're sick of their data being sold behind their backs and of being quietly duped into buying a shoddy product. Much of the business ethos over the past fifty years has been about tricking the customer or spinning the story, and at its worst, it has been bold-faced lies. Historically, under few circumstances would a company own up to a mistake or genuinely do the right thing because it was the right thing to do. The customer had to accept that behavior because they had no power and there often weren't other options, so they couldn't hold the business accountable. Now, the customer has all the power. Today and moving forward, you must live up to who you say you are or else the customer will leave you behind with no remorse. You have to communicate who you are and what your value is—with no bullshit—and then you have to live up to that commitment. You can only control your half of the relationship, so make damn sure you're honest, caring, and loving, or you'll be kicked to the curb.

A breach of the customer's trust can impact your business instantaneously. If you lie, break trust, or otherwise suck in any way, it won't take long for people to know. Word of mouth used to travel slowly as your customers physically moved about, and the impact was relatively slight because the only people they could tell were those in front of them. The impact of a positive or negative experience stayed in the forefront of the brain perhaps a few days and reached a few dozen people at most.

Today, if one of your customers has a bad experience with your business, they can and will let people know about it through mediums that are lightning fast. You can be called out on social media in front of thousands of people almost instantly. Don't put yourself in that situation. If you do find yourself there, treat that customer with respect, honesty, and humility. Address their concerns by apologizing, offering a solution, and thanking them for the frank feedback. Then make sure it doesn't happen again.

It is scary that they can communicate negativity so quickly, but remember, they can also communicate *positivity* that efficiently. I personally love this new world of shareable information and electronic networking, because if you are running an outstanding, trustworthy business, people are going to tell others about it. You will instantly stand out from the crowd.

The power of this is staggering, so make sure every customer's experience is a positive one.

In my opinion, authenticity is one of the most powerful changes in business during the past half century. Recently, my wife and I were discussing this very topic, and my nine-year-old daughter asked a few questions. She was mostly concerned about what happens if a customer becomes angry and how you recover if you screw up.

The power of our exchange became evident a few days later, when my wife sent me a text with the quote from my daughter, "We aren't the fastest, we aren't the cheapest, but at least you know you can trust us." She was talking about starting a moving company, and frankly, I think she is on to something. If I am hiring a company to move my worldly possessions across the country, I am not necessarily interested in it being the fastest or even the cheapest. The one thing I want in a moving company is honesty and the ability to believe that they will protect my treasures. Above all else, I need to believe they'll do what they say they are going to do.

It's the same with any other business. Don't try to deceive your customers; they're too smart, and it will always backfire. Give them an authentically great product and an authentic, stellar customer experience. Then, when they tag you on Twitter, their hundreds of followers are hundreds of potential new customers.

INJECT THE WORLD WITH POSITIVE ENERGY. NOBODY WANTS TO HANG OUT WITH A LOSER!

Finally, *faith*, *confidence*, and *courage* are words you don't hear often when it comes to business. Sure, you have to have faith that your business will take off. You have to be confident in your product, and you have to have the courage to start a business in the first place. A lot of it. I will also tell you that the type and tone of your aura is absolutely critical to your overall success. Huh?

This is one of the great lessons I learned from my business partner, Bob Fish. Over the years, we have faced a number of difficult times. We struggled. We complained. Our attitude would be less than pleasant in private, but to the outside world, the business was always doing great—not because we lied about it to ourselves or anyone else when we struggled, but because we believed in the business and knew we'd get through. We always demonstrated faith and confidence. Looking back on it now, it was one of the most crucial elements to get to where we are today. Even if we were on the brink of bankruptcy, we knew, we always believed, the business would work and that it was going to succeed in a big way.

Bob's belief in the business is infectious. If I had a dollar for every time he left a meeting room having filled everyone in attendance with an amazing amount of confidence in us, our company, and our brand, I'd never have to sell another cup of coffee again (but I would anyway). It was awesome to watch. It simply came down to the fact that our company was going to succeed. We were going to realize our goals and our objectives, and nothing was going to stop us, even with some pretty harsh realities along the way. I remember a number of conversations over the years when Bob would be frustrated because people didn't believe. They had doubts about what we were doing, and it showed, but he was always able to bring them around.

If you have doubts, so will everyone else. Your attitude is up to one person and one person only: you. The customer—and, therefore, your new business—will live and die by your attitude. If you have a wonderfully positive attitude, the world will buy into what you are doing and, more importantly, buy what you are selling.

I have watched this scenario play out many times in my career of helping people start businesses. When we sign up a new owner into our system, they are always positive. It is new and exciting, and they're ready to start the most successful coffee shop the world has ever seen. Throughout the opening process, however, things can get tough, and I can begin to sense what their attitude will be in more normal circumstances.

The real answer comes when we do a follow-up call to the owner forty-five days into their operation. That is the call when I know if they are going to make it or not. At this point, over twenty years and well over 200 stores in, I wish I had taken notes and made predictions, because I am pretty sure my evaluation of their attitude at forty-five days would be a great predictor of their future success. They are all tired. They all have stories about the process and how frustrating it has been. The vast majority of the stores are underperforming based on what the operator expected, and they are typically worried. That's all normal. But it is their reaction to those circumstances that is telling. Some are defeatist and make excuses. They complain about external circumstances. At times, the finger is pointed squarely at us, as if we tricked them into investing in our concept.

I always struggle emotionally at that moment. Empathy sets in like a ton of bricks. I used to try to placate them or cheer them up. I would explain that it is typical and that it is going to get better. They just needed to follow the system. They needed to keep at it, and it would turn around. The problem with this approach was that it wasn't the truth.

Over time, I have adjusted my approach to be as authentic with them as I can be. Now, when I have the opportunity to engage an owner with a negative attitude at this stage of development, I simply lay out the truth: I am worried for them, and I am quite sure that they aren't going to make it if this is their attitude. They had better figure out how to get out of the negative swamp they are wallowing in or their days are numbered. In all of my years, I have only seen a negative operator turn into a great, successful operator a few times. Once you are riding on the negative bus, it is difficult to get off. I explain that nobody in the world can change their attitude but them. It will be the biggest challenge they face in developing their new business, but they're the only one who can do it.

On the flip side of that coin, we talk to many positive owners forty-five days into their new business, and these are the ones I know can succeed. They are tired too. Typically, the business isn't meeting their expectations either; it takes awhile to build a customer base. As we mentioned previously, people frequently go into business with expectations that result in disappointment. But this pool of operators, the positive ones, are committed to growing their business. They aren't making excuses. They are talking about all of the things they are doing to build revenue. They have had difficult times like everyone, but they understand that is part of the journey. They understand they are on a steep learning curve, and they are asking for advice on how to do it better, what they must do to improve. Nine times out of ten with these folks, the answer is to keep doing what they are doing, and it will work out. They believe me, they do what they are challenged to do, and in the end, it works.

Your faith, confidence, and courage are mission critical to your organization. I have never read authors of business books promoting a positive attitude. I have never heard a business class taught on the power of positive mental energy. But as corny as it may sound, when you are positive, you attract positivity. The more positivity you attract, the more attractive you are as a business, and the more likely you will grow and thrive. It is a self-fulfilling prophecy. Don't let anyone change you or your attitude. Stay as positive as the day you made the commitment to open the business, and keep the dream alive.

HAPPINESS IS BRINGING JOY TO OTHERS

This may be an argument most would consider to be misplaced in a business book: if you bring joy to people—if you bring love to people—they are going to naturally love you back.

Many, many businesspeople I deal with are jaded and cynical. They are tired, beaten down. Their new business has gone from being a dream of independence and wealth to simply making a mediocre paycheck. I wish I had the ability to send them back through time, to the days just before they opened their businesses, and show them to themselves. They were full of hope. They were going to set the world on fire. They were going to be the best at what they were doing. Today, they are defeated. They hate the world, and they feel that the world hates them back.

I had an acquaintance when I was younger who was an inspiration to me—a mentor. He was a pilot and a cowboy entrepreneur (the kind from the business books of old: the guy who chewed on nails and worked people to the bone with little remorse, who didn't give a shit what people thought of him, who was cocksure and taking on the world), and every bone in my body wanted to be like him when I grew up. He was tough, didn't care what people thought, and was very successful. Once, I recall him advising a friend of mine to get a good job like an engineer for a large company, do good work, and save for retirement. He advised that trying to be an entrepreneur wasn't worth it, because it had become too difficult to make any money. There were just too many regulations, and if you did figure out how to make money, it all went to taxes anyway. You know the old rich man syndrome: things today are different, too difficult; if they had to do it all over again, they probably wouldn't. Customers had gotten so difficult that they made it almost impossible to stay in business anymore. Back in the day, you could make an honest dollar; now, he was not sure.

I remember just shaking my head. Here he was the lead character in the storybook about America and entrepreneurship, and now he was complaining that there was no money to be made while driving in his Ferrari to the airport to fly his private plane? Why would someone so successful be so jaded?

In my opinion, you become jaded when you lose sight of the fact that building a business is hard. If it were easy, everyone would be doing it. On a regular basis, when I get frustrated with my business or with people associated with my business, I have to remind myself that, yes, what I do is difficult, but I also get compensated well for it, and the freedom and benefits are beyond compare.

Recently, I spent an afternoon with two men who had sold their businesses in the previous twelve months. They both did quite well, one in the deep eight figures and the other well into nine figures. Neither of these guys ever has to work again.

I asked one of them, "What has been the biggest surprise for you now that you are a few months removed from the day-to-day action?"

His reply was priceless: "I was in complete denial about how much pressure I was under. I thought I was handling it all really well, but I didn't know how heavy it was until it was gone."

You're going to be exhausted and stressed and strapped for cash, especially at the start. But don't lose sight of this fact: you and your business are magical. You are making an awesome product or performing a crucial service (because that's the point, remember?). You delight people with delicious coffee or the perfect algorithm or the newest and healthiest deodorant. Your business is a powerful force in the world with the potential to bring joy to other people—not only to your customers, but also to all of your employees and then all of the people your employees touch daily.

I love the book *If You Want to Write* by Brenda Ueland, which is anything but a book on business. Guy Kawasaki—a leading thinker, writer, and speaker in the arena of entrepreneurialism—recommended the book to me. It was inspirational for sure. Following are just a few powerful insights I took away from her book about creativity and how to tackle big projects. So much of it translates into a business start-up. These are the words I wrote in the margins, the things I was inspired to consider while reading her book:

- You must be motivated to delight people—to impress them, to want them to love you and your business. If not, what is the point?

- Imagine if everyone started a business with the goal of delighting other people. If every day we all woke up and worked with the goal of impressing and delighting each other. What a splendid place the world would be. We all get extraordinary joy from delighting others. Why, then, does it happen so rarely?[1]

I acknowledge that I am taking her thoughts one step further outside of the realm she was considering, but I think they apply perfectly, and they inspired me to consider using the word *love* when talking about the relationship between you and your customers. I think the great businesses, the great start-ups, inspire a feeling of love between themselves and their customers. One of the strongest ways to build your business is to make sure you are focused on bringing joy every minute of every day. When you

---

1   Brenda Ueland, *If You Want to Write* (Martino Fine Books, 2011).

get this, the success of your start-up will be a forgone conclusion, and you will be on your way to building a thriving company.

This goes back to making your customers love you. No one wants to date a stick in the mud. They want to be with someone who brings them joy and happiness every day, and they'll want to return the favor.

LIFELONG COMMITMENT TO RELATIONSHIPS

Your business is more than your relationship with your customers. It is about your relationship with anyone your business touches. You have to build strong connections with your partners, your suppliers, your bank—everybody. But most crucially, you have to make your customers fall head over heels in love with you.

My dad has been going to the same breakfast joint for twenty-five years. He knows the waitresses. He knows their kids' names and even where they go to school. He remembers when the restaurant changed cooks three years ago and what a difficult transition it was. My dad is perfectly loyal, and for good reason: his diner is awesome. The food is good, and the service is great. But that's only part of the story. They care about him, too. The first time I went with him, the waitress knew my name before I introduced myself. They know about his job and what's important to him. They care. They've become a part of his history and of his life. I love going there now too, and even better, I love going there with him.

If you opened a new shiny diner across the street, with a

modernized menu, better parking, and cleaner bathrooms, do you think my dad would give you a try? Not a chance in the world! In fact, over my dad's dead body would he walk into the new joint. He would be worried about *his* people in *his* diner. He'd worry that business might slow down and that the people he cares about would struggle.

The diner and my dad have built a relationship over decades based on authentic empathy and delicious food. You need to be that diner: love your customers. Be authentic with them. Do whatever it takes to get them into your "shop," then keep them there by building trust and affection. And offer the best damn coffee or (insert your core product) they'll ever have. When their colleagues and their friends and their kids all start coming into your shop, you'll know you've done it right.

I remember conversations over the years with family members of some of our loyal customers. They would talk about how obsessed their mom, brother, aunt, or best friend was with our coffee, so they just had to come give it a try. This was always the greatest form of praise I could receive. Without a doubt, we would double down to provide this family member a mind-blowing experience. Often, I would buy their coffee for them on their first visit, telling them I love their mom, brother, aunt, or best friend so much that the coffee was on me. They walked out maybe not quite loving me, but definitely crushing on me and my business.

It is simple to understand why anyone in business would like a lifelong relationship with the customer. I will never forget the conversation I had with one customer. I asked her how she had heard about our business. She said her brother drove a

UPS truck, and one day he was raving about how amazing and fun the BIGGBY home office (corporate) he delivered to was each and every day. She decided to try the local BIGGBY store in her town. She has been a loyalist ever since. We treated the UPS driver with respect and loved all over him when he was in our store. In turn, he became a promoter of our business. I don't know if this guy ever bought a latte from us, but his sister bought many. For many in business, the UPS driver would just be the UPS driver, but in our world he became a promoter; he loved us, and we loved him. That is how we are with everybody.

Vendors can become strong promoters of the business as well. Not only can they promote your business, but when you have a good long-standing relationship, a lifelong relationship, your vendor is going to take care of you at every opportunity. Many times, vendors have gone over and above for us when we were in a pinch because they knew we were going to be a customer for decades to come. Maybe they will take a large bill and put it out over time for you to help you with the short-term cash pinch. Maybe they are willing to invest in a piece of equipment to help enhance your core product. It is $150k, but that is OK. They know they will recoup the investment because you are going to be a customer for many years.

Many times over the years, my lawyer has leaned across the table and whispered, "Mike, I'm not advising you as my client right now, I am advising you as I would my brother . . . " Whenever this happens, I pay close attention. This is the kind of advice she isn't giving to everyone. She is doing this because she genuinely cares about me and our business. We have worked together for going on twenty years. She is my lawyer.

Chapter 5

BE CONSISTENTLY, PERFECTLY COMMITTED

ON MORE THAN ONE OCCASION while growing my start-up, I was accused of wanting too much. I was told my expectations were too high and that perfection was impossible. At one of these moments, I realized perfection was the only expectation, the only thing I wanted—and I erupted.

I asked, "If we were in a war with ground troops in battles in seventeen locations and thousands of lives depended on our proper execution, would we give up on half of those locations, or would we try to protect all of them? Wouldn't we strive for perfection with people's lives on the line?"

In that situation, my expectation would seem quite reasonable. And my new business was that important to me—like a battle with lives on the line. I had to succeed. There was no choice. It was life and death for me—period. I wasn't *kind of* doing my business; I was all in, 100 percent committed. And if you weren't available for that level of commitment, you weren't welcome to join the fight. Over the years, I have rounded off some of the sharp edges of that attitude, but the sentiment wasn't wrong. During start-up, it is life or death for your business. You succeed, or it dies. There is no middle ground.

One of our early employees was known to be a little iffy on procedure. It wasn't just one area but a little slop here and a little slop there. No single mistake was enough for her to be fired or even reprimanded, but each missed detail added to the whole. For example, when we're working the register, our procedure is to put all the bills in the till facing the same direction. That might seem overly nitpicky, but the next cashier might pause for a moment to readjust the bills as they give out change; they might even miscount because the bills don't look the same. One pause or one missing dollar might not seem like much, but seconds add up to hours, and single dollars add up to thousands over time.

The same is true for any procedure. Maybe someone on the closing crew needs to leave and doesn't clean the espresso machine. That means the next morning's crew has to clean it. While they're cleaning the equipment, they're not prepping the store to open. Maybe it takes them ten minutes to finish cleaning and balance the register before they open the door. In that time, a half-dozen customers have walked up, pulled on the locked door, and then walked around the corner to the next coffee shop. That's six lost sales for that day alone, and those customers might never come back. That cumulative lost revenue can kill a start-up.

Instead, strive for perfection. If your employee has to leave before she finishes the closing duties list, you have to stay and finish it. Better yet, get her started early so she finishes before she has to leave. Every procedure must be followed every time, every dollar counted, every coffee made perfectly, and every customer satisfied. Perfection is an insurmountable goal, but you do have to reach for it. If you aren't always striving for perfection, there is a moving target. My experience with moving targets is they typically slide in the wrong direction over time. Perfect is perfect.

In my experience, many people struggle with perfection. It is exhausting, and to be perfect means you never shut down, never take a break from the intensity. It's easy to drop this one thing just this one time, but it's never only one thing or one time. However, part of paying attention to these details—and making sure they're perfect—is realizing the benefits they bring with them. That clean espresso machine means the morning crew can get right to work opening the store. That open door means half a dozen coffees sold and half a dozen satisfied—potential repeat—customers.

Early on in the development of the company, we were courted by a private equity firm. We had shown incredible growth and were technically out of the start-up phase at that point. The founder of the firm had taken a personal interest in our company and was eager to make the investment. In the end, we decided against the deal, but in the process, I had the opportunity to ask one of his people why he was so invested in making this deal happen.

She laughed a little and said, "It was the syrup bottles."

Early in the negotiations, when we were first getting to know each other, we had a meeting in our training center—essentially, a practice café built into our office space. As we talked, the investment guy watched one of our employees methodically wipe down all twenty-five syrup pumps and bottles, as she was following our late-afternoon closing procedures for the training center. We weren't even in an operational store, there wasn't a training session happening, but a system was being followed: the syrup bottles needed to be wiped down at close each day, so our employee wiped them down. For us, it was simply what we do, nothing special. We were executing, and executing as close to perfect as possible. For the investor, it was eureka. He wanted to be part of a company that paid that close attention to detail.

If I have said it once, I have said it a thousand times, and I need to say it again: your relationships are your business. You have to constantly build trust with your customers, your employees, and your community. Striving for perfection creates that trust by showing your customers that you'll deliver what they expect every time. It shows your employees that you are doing exactly what you expect of them and makes those expectations clear. Even if you're not feeling perfect, you can reach, you can improve, and you can fight for the life of your business every day.

PERFECT CONSISTENCY

As the general manager of our second store, I opened the doors every morning. The shop was in a building in downtown Lansing, and I wanted to avoid having anyone show up to the store and see it in that dead, flat state a retail store emanates when it is closed. I wanted to be a beacon of energy and life for our customers every single morning. My concern was that people would have a different time set on their watches or in their cars, their clock set a few minutes fast, and they'd arrive before we opened. So I made sure to turn the "Open" sign on three hundred seconds before we opened. For the first year, I would stand at the switch, looking at my watch and waiting for the exact moment before lighting the neon. The rest of the opening crew knew they had to have everything ready before that moment, that we were going to open at the same time—down to the second—every day. This sent a clear message: we are going to execute perfectly.

Perfection gives you a baseline. If you execute perfectly, everyone—your team and your customers—has clear expectations. Once the crew is on board with perfection, you can start to tweak the procedure or policy, and your changes will affect the business. For example, if you open your store three hundred seconds before the official open time and you start to notice that there are three or four people waiting for you every morning, you can make the decision to open six hundred seconds early or even take the drastic step of changing your hours to open thirty minutes earlier.

However, consistency is crucial. If you open three hundred seconds early one day, on time the next day, sixty seconds late another day, and so forth, you wouldn't ever have the opportunity to learn whether people are interested in your being open earlier. Worse, if on a given day you opened on time and disappointed the customers who were arriving three hundred seconds early, they're not likely to show up three hundred seconds early tomorrow. And they might go somewhere else instead. *Perfection* means being perfect in your execution—every time. Your customers need to trust you, and your employees need to know what to expect from you and what you expect from them. That only comes with perfect consistency.

In my experience, when you expect great things of people, when you expect perfection, they will live up to your expectation and perform. People want to be successful. They want to do a great job. They simply need to know what they need to do in order to do a great job! If you expect greatness, you will get greatness. If you expect mediocre, you will get mediocre.

But remember: you're the example. In start-up mode, if you let one detail slide, you communicate to your team that perfection isn't important. They see you fudging the edges, so they have no incentive to reach for perfect themselves.

Most business owners I engage with have a less-than-stellar opinion of their people. To me, this is just silly and backward. Your staff will live up to the expectations you set. If you expect them to be bad at their jobs, they'll be bad at their jobs; if you think they are amazing, they will amaze you.

DEPENDABLE, BY DEFINITION, MEANS *EVERY TIME*

My business partner is about as obsessive as they come. It is one of the reasons why I was so attracted to working with him. He constantly strives for perfection and expects it from everyone around him. I took this as a challenge. When we first started working together, I told myself, *I can never screw up in front of him.* To this day, twenty years later, we maintain this dynamic. If we are meeting in a hotel lobby for dinner, nine times out of ten we both arrive at the exact moment we agreed on—not a minute late. It is rare that something happens other than exactly what we are expecting to happen. That is a lovely way to live—confident in expectations. Give that confidence to everyone you work with.

When you are consistent, your customers and employees need to know that you are there for them and that you and your business are going to live up to your commitments. This is a fundamental concept and critical to your success. You have told them who you are going to be and what you are going to deliver; now you have to live up to that expectation by delivering perfectly every time—no exceptions. In start-up, this is on you, period.

Just take a moment to reflect on the complexity of being dependable to everyone in your business and contrast that with being dependable as an employee. As an employee, you must be dependable to one person: your boss. There is only one lens you look through to determine and rate your dependability: their opinion.

As a manager of your new business, you need to be dependable through many different lenses. Your customers have to see you as dependable by providing your goods or service in a consistent manner. You must be dependable to your team: the people working for you are trusting you with their lives and their futures. There are also vendors and other stakeholders. Don't forget your local community as a whole, the larger ecosystem we all depend on. Are you ready to be accountable to each of these bodies? If not, or if you think you can sidestep your responsibility to any of them, you will soon learn the power each brings to bear on your start-up.

I know this sounds harsh, like too much responsibility. It may be overwhelming to consider, but I make this point for one reason: to ensure you understand that starting a business does not give you more freedom; it weighs you down more than you understand today. So, I hope I am poking one last hole in the mystical magical balloon of personal freedom. If you are starting your business because you are tired of working inside of a structure that holds you accountable, tired of working long hours, and want flexibility and freedom . . . that can happen, but your business will need to cross many, many thresholds of success before it does. In my opinion, you are looking at seven to ten years after start-up, if ever. One of the key factors most people underestimate is how long it takes.

It is critical that you are prepared for the race. It isn't as simple as the hare versus the tortoise. The hare can run faster than the tortoise for a few moments, because it has to be able to outmaneuver a big cat or dog from time to time, but it can't keep up that pace. The key is to know when to sprint, when to run, when to jog, and when to walk.

When I was a young hockey player, maybe ten or twelve years old, a coach pulled me aside. He said something like, "Mike, your energy and effort levels are great. But they're getting in the way of you becoming a better hockey player. You skate as fast as you can all of the time. The problem is, the defender knows how fast you will be going. You need to vary your speed. The most important thing isn't the effort level you are giving; it is knowing when to apply maximum effort and when to coast and relax and let the play unfold in front of you."

I became a much better hockey player with that advice, and it works in business, too. Sometimes in business, you have to let the play unfold in front of you. Relax, take a breather, so when the next opportunity to sprint presents itself, you are ready to take advantage.

Sometimes different parties depending on you could have competing needs. For example, you are committed to the health and vitality of your team. One of your team members may run smack dab into a personal crisis that is outside of their control. Let's say your sales manager has a sick child and her husband is out of the country, traveling for work. You get the call at one a.m. that she won't be able to be at the airport at six thirty to board a plane for a critical sales meeting with a large potential client. You and your sales manager are the only two people qualified to give the presentation. Boom, there it is. You roll out of bed, start packing your bag, and begin doing the prep work for the presentation in the morning. Everything on your docket at work, plus your kid's soccer games—everything for the next two days—is scratched. Your team is depending on you to take care of them in times of need, and your customers need to know they can depend on you to deliver. Therefore, canceling that sales meeting or presentation in early-stage development of your start-up is simply not an option. This is clearly a moment in start-up when you need to sprint. Pacing yourself at other times allows you to be prepared to sprint when necessary. You can't sprint all of the time. It is a marathon for sure, with many intermittent sprints called for spontaneously. To be perfect, you might spend days in a sprint not knowing when the pace will slow down. Be ready.

You have to be the most dedicated and dependable person within your business forever. As I have said, many people go into business thinking it is going to give them personal freedom. They won't have a boss, so they think they'll be able to do whatever they want, whenever they want. There is a morsel of truth here, but there is also the flip side of the coin: if you plan on being the most dedicated and dependable person in the business for the first seven to ten years, your personal liberation won't manifest for a very long time. Why? When you have a boss, the boss has the ability to let you off the hook. The boss can tell you to take a few days off and recover from a particularly stressful event. You walk out free of mind and secure in your place in the business. You are doing a great job, and the boss recognizes it and recommends a respite. When you own a business, there is no getting off the hook. If you are committed to the success of your business, it will own you and your calendar. There is no boss to set you free.

Owning a business is about personal freedom in the end, but it is the long game. For three days in a row, this very week I have awoken between two and four o'clock a.m. after three to five hours of sleep. Why? Because I have things on my mind, I am beholden to the organization, I have to get certain things done, and I have a hard time sleeping when deadlines loom. I wake up because I care deeply about the organization and, more importantly, the people in it. I am twenty-three years into the business, and BIGGBY COFFEE will sell $130 million at retail this year. We are well established and stable. Is this personal freedom?

IN A START-UP, VENDORS ARE YOUR PARTNERS/INVESTORS

Let's take a quick look at vendors. Vendors are strategic partners in your growth. There are countless times during start-up that a vendor will need to step in and go over the top to help take care of you and, therefore, your customer. If a vendor is not willing to do so, you could be left for dead. The only way a vendor is willing to do so is if they trust you and know you are going to take care of them in the long term. This seems so simple, and yet it is astonishing how often I hear of business owners talking about and treating vendors as adversaries. Sure, a vendor doesn't want to lose your business, but the fact of the matter is that during start-up you are small, and therefore you don't represent much of their revenue pie. In the beginning, they will do the bare minimum to keep your business unless they believe in your greatness, you are an opportunity.

A close friend of mine was the chairman and CEO of a historic national brand that is traded on the New York Stock Exchange. He left his position as CEO of this company and ventured into a primarily self-funded start-up. I remember talking to him at one point, and he laughed when referencing a meeting he had with his PR firm. He said something like:

> When I was a CEO, I used to walk into their office and they would have the red carpet laid out. In the conference

room would be the creative director, their CEO, and three or four account reps waiting to take notes and handle my every need. When I walked in as the founder of my start-up, I literally had a junior account rep and an intern available to me. The CEO didn't even stop in to say hello.

My point here is, when you are big, you have all the resources; when you are in start-up, the resources made available to you are often minimal—at least until you prove yourself.

Over time, as you grow, treat them with respect, and live up to your commitments, you will find they become willing to make investments in your business. They become a fuel source for you eventually, but this relationship begins during start-up. The sooner you demonstrate how dependable you are, the sooner they trust you and are willing to invest in you.

We have always had a wonderful relationship with one of our key partners, our coffee roaster. Early on, they were willing to make strategic investments. We have always been dedicated to them and to their business as well. We support them by making sure they get paid, by accepting their analysis of their cost structure, and by trying to make sure our pricing is acceptable to them. Even more important has been transparency around our needs. Over the years, we have considered switching to different roasters and have come close a few times. There have always been strategic reasons for our consideration, but we have always brought our concerns to the table and talked about why we were considering a change. This has consistently provided them the opportunity to fill that need. Lo and behold, twenty years later we are still buying coffee from them. They are dependable and trustworthy, and they live up to their commitments. We are dependable, trustworthy, and we live up to our commitments. They cherish us and our business and have supported us in countless ways, hundreds of times over the years. We cherish them as a partner in our growth.

Early on, we had the opportunity to buy a retail operation of six coffee shops. It was a monumental deal at our stage of the business, and it was going to elevate us to a different level of sophistication. We were young, barely cash flowing if at all, and we had little in the way of capital to invest. Our roaster was willing to lend us one-sixth of the total capital to pull off the acquisition via debt in a second position to our primary lender. We put a sixth of the investment in equity, and we brought in a fifty-fifty partner to put their sixth in equity and leveraged up, and the bank took the other half, three-sixths. Our roaster was willing to do this because they knew us. They knew our character, and they believed we would live up to our commitments.

I referenced this deal earlier in the book, and you may remember that eighteen months into operation, the bank put us in default. This meant we couldn't make payments to our vendor because they were in a second position. Instead of making the bank the bad guy and telling our roaster there was nothing we could do, we went to the mat with the bank and ended up a blood-stained mess because we simply wouldn't walk away from our commitment to our roaster. It was horrible and painful, but we stood by our vendor as aggressively as possible. In the end, we worked it all out and everyone got paid.

In a later meeting, we were bestowed one of the great

honors from the CEO of our vendor when he referred to my partner and me as *mensches* (people of integrity and honor). As I sit here today, this vendor is willing to make enormous strategic investments in the growth and health of our business. This began in start-up mode because we lived up to our commitments and always respected them by having "real" conversations. We wouldn't be the company we are today without their partnership.

YOU ARE AN ACTOR, AND YOU MUST GIVE THE PERFORMANCE OF YOUR LIFE

It is squarely on your shoulders to convince people, to get them to believe in you and your business. People are taking a risk by supporting you, and if you can't convince them of your potential, your business will never get traction, and your start-up will fail. You have to be a winner for your business to be a winner. People want to be with and will always associate with a winner. When you are in start-up, you are just entering the gates of viability, so it is up to you to create that aura within your organization. If people perceive you as beaten, then you are beaten. Once this happens, you should just throw in the towel; it is over.

This is so much harder than most people consider. During start-up you will get kicked in the teeth time and time again. Unless you win the lottery or open that one-in-a-million business that produces cash flow consistently from the beginning, you will be out of cash for many, many months—even years—during start-up. Juggling cash at the beginning is like somebody knowing they are going to need blood throughout a surgical procedure or they will die—so the doctor asks them to juggle quarts of blood in glass jars as the procedure is happening. If they drop a quart, their chance of survival diminishes. Their body is cut open, a doctor is monkeying around inside of them, and they are expected to juggle fragile jars of blood. Dramatic? Yes, but this is as close an analogy as I can find for managing cash during start-up. There is so much pressure.

In your personal life, if you run out of cash, there is credit available everywhere. In business, the second you are in negative cash flow, the cash dries up and becomes one of the most scarce commodities on earth. Let me assure you that until you are out of start-up and cash is flowing in your business, your ability to get cash relies on your ability to get personal loans from those closest to you, or your ability to generate gross margin through revenue generation. The exception might be in Silicon Valley where you are working on some new world-beating technology, and people are willing to invest money based on very different metrics than the standard position the rest of the world lives by: cash flow!

There are few things in the world that put someone under the same kind of pressure as being out of cash. You will most likely be tight on cash, balancing pennies like a magician. It is tough, and for many it feels like a great deal of strain. But the world cannot know, especially your staff or your customers. This is one of the hardest things you will face in your start-up. You will have to be all things to all people concurrently. Even when you are out of cash!

Example: You are a few months into your start-up, and you are negative cash flowing, literally managing your cash on a daily basis. It is eight a.m., and a key employee—that person you had confidence in; that person you were thinking about making a manager; that person who was going to take some of the workload off your shoulders—resigns because she is moving to Florida with her boyfriend. She loves the job and loves working with you, but she has to follow her dreams, and they have decided their dream is to live near the ocean. Another employee interrupts the tear-filled hug to tell you one of your key machines is down and production is at a standstill. (By the way, before starting your business, you were about as mechanically handy as a giraffe, and now you are grabbing your toolbox and making a beeline to the broken equipment.) You get that fire out, and your mom calls you to let you know one of the kids is complaining of a sore throat, and she is wondering whether she should take your youngest to school.

You look in the mirror in the hall as you get off the phone with your mother, and you look like death warmed over. There is a smudge of dirt on your forehead. You have grime under your fingernails, and your hair looks like you brushed it with an egg beater. You stop in the bathroom, splash some water on your face, wash your hands, run your fingers through your hair, and walk into the conference room five minutes late with a potential game-changing customer who asks, "How is it going? How is business?" The potential customer in the conference wants to know how you are holding up. It's a similar series of questions that you get in the first six months of your baby's life. They expect you to be miserable. They expect you to be exhausted. They know the odds are stacked against you. They won't say it, but they are expecting you to fail.

To make your business successful, you must walk through the door of your conference room and give the performance of your life. The potential customer must feel like this thing is going well—better than you expected. (This is not a lie because they have no idea what your expectation was; maybe you were expecting to lose $17,000 per month and you are only losing $14,000.) You are very happy with your business and ecstatic over the decision to leave your cushy corporate job to go it on your own. You are having a hard time keeping up with production. This is not a lie because the machines keep breaking down, not because there is too much business. It is your mission to make sure the customer leaves the meeting with the utmost confidence in you and your business.

Even if they leave the meeting with great confidence in you and what you are doing, the chances you are going to win the business are still low. If they leave with any doubts about you or your business, your chances go to zero. By the way, did I mention that this is your fourth sales call this week and your fourteenth this month, and that your win ratio is running at about one in twenty? The meeting wraps up, and you feel like it went well. You shake hands with your prospects, reach into your pocket, get your phone out, and start scrolling through voice mails as they walk away.

There is a voice mail from a customer who is irate over some packaging issue; another from the banker, who is wondering about two checks that hit your account NSF (non-sufficient funds); and a third from your key vendor, who has a box of critical raw materials ready to ship over but realized your account is past due, and he needs payment before he can ship.

You call the vendor back as you walk into the break room, and you let him know you are expecting a large payment any day and you are going to get the overdue payments cleared up Monday of next week. You exude energy and enthusiasm. You spend a few minutes talking about the sales call you just came out of, which is "gonna be a real game changer for the company." You have been very good at communicating with him over the past six months. You have shared the highs and the lows with him, and he feels like a partner in your start-up. He knows that when you grow the business, he stands to flourish from this account. You have lived up to your other commitments, and he sees no reason not to believe that you will wire the money on Monday. He takes a chance and sends the materials anyway, even though it is against his company's policy. Of course, you thank him and tell him how good he has been to you and how you look forward to doing business with him for many years to come. He gets off the phone feeling good about your business and feeling even better about you. He is contributing to the success of a start-up. He is your partner.

You walk into the break room, and there are a gaggle of employees hanging out talking about the ducks that walked into the back of the building through the garage door earlier that morning. They are in a good mood and joking about how the grumpy old codger who drives the forklift had to beep his horn to get the ducks out of the way, and even he smiled and gave a little chuckle at the notion. You walk in talking about the sales call and how invigorating it was because it truly could be a game changer. This was the second meeting with them, and you think it went better than the first. You go check in on the machine that was broken earlier in the morning and give the operator a high five because the machine is still working. Your people seem fired up; they are in it with you, and they know it is tough at the moment, but they believe in you and what you are doing. They speak highly of you and your company to the UPS driver, to their friends at dinner on Friday night, to their kids, and most importantly, to each other. They are fired up and have confidence because you are fired up and have confidence Your people have confidence in you and your business. And yet . . . you remember your kid is home sick and you call to check in. It never ends. It never stops. You just have to put your head down and keep going.

You are acting. You must decide what is the most appropriate behavior for you at any given moment, and you must morph into that character. If you had walked into the sales call with grime under your fingernails, talking about the broken equipment, or if you had left the conference room and walked into the break room complaining about the vendor who didn't ship, or if you had been on the phone with the vendor talking about all of the misses on sales calls in the past month, people would be walking away with little or no confidence in you or the business. You have to inject them with positive energy; you have to fill them with belief. You do this by being a great actor. You must flip the switch in every situation and know what you need to do to set the tone for that moment. You must have people walk away with no doubt about the success of your enterprise.

This is harder to do than many people think because internally you are going through hell. To act like everything is amazing when your head is in the jaws of the alligator takes an amazing actor. I remember the relief I used to feel when I worked at the office in the evenings or on a weekend during start-up. It was a relief because I could work without having to be acting at the same time. Nobody was watching body language, nobody was listening to my conversation, and I didn't have the second job of being a Broadway performer while trying to run the business. When you are there with all of your people and the curtain closes at the end of the day, you have to be able to walk to your dressing room, sit down in front of your mirror, and know that you just gave the performance of your life.

CRAZY, DEMENTED, KOOKY, INSANE, NUTS, PSYCHO, UNHINGED, MANIACAL, DIPPY, DERANGED

There are so many moments in the development of your business in which you can choose to take the easy road or continue to drive the boat as fast as you possibly can. Remember, start-up is a race. From the day you open the business, you are in a race to get to your first day of cash flow. The race boat is leaking water like a bucket with holes drilled in the bottom. You are at the helm, there is wind gusting between thirty and forty miles per hour, the waves are bigger than mounds of snow in a Walmart parking lot in January (in Michigan, of course), you may have just seen a water spout in your periphery, and you are not sure if it is going to hit you . . . Well then, stay on course. You have the engine wide open, banging on wave after wave. You have weather lines up, and everyone above deck is tethered in because it is almost impossible to walk. Visibility is zero. It is freezing cold. Your first mate walks up to you with a worried look, like maybe you are pushing a little too hard. You look him right in the eye and exclaim, "Isn't this amazing! Just about the coolest thing I have ever done. Hold on tight, big boy; we are about to hit another" as you crash face-first into another monster wave. Here is the rub: you mean it. You are loving it. This race is the greatest thing you have ever done. It is what you always wanted!

To be realistic, not every day will be like juggling quarts of blood during surgery or like driving your boat at full speed through a monsoon. But some will, and it is how you respond at these moments that will determine your fate in start-up. When you look your first mate in the eye and say, "Isn't this amazing?" and mean it, you set the tone. Everyone involved with your organization will take note and understand that you will do whatever it takes for the business to succeed. Everyone in the organization will feed off you and your commitment. They will support you and pull really hard for your success.

Let me try to make one more comparison that is probably inappropriate and may get me in trouble with some moms out there: your business is like a newborn baby. The infant is dependent on Mom. Other people are involved, of course, and helping out, but for the most part, the baby is interested in being with Mom. In this scenario, the business is the infant, and the founder of the business is Mom. The needs of the baby are immense and all consuming. The baby doesn't care if Mom is having a bad day or exhausted with two other kids hanging on her for their needs.

As of this writing, we have a new baby in our household. There are times when I don't know how my wife does it. I know she is exhausted and at her wits' end, but when the baby needs something, she approaches him with love and care and provides anything and everything for him. There are even times when I offer to help and she responds, "No, no, I got it. I want to." She is tired and drained and running on empty, but I know if you asked her, she would tell you it is amazing and truly a great honor. She knows her efforts today are going to pay off for our little boy down the road. It is worth the investment; it is worth the time; it is worth the effort.

The emotional intensity will not be the same in your business as with a baby, but the energy and effort will be similar. The main difference between a baby and your business is that the baby cries. It has that built-in mechanism to let you know when it is in need. As a parent, you also have an inherent instinctual trigger to care for the baby. Your business will not cry, and you don't have an instinctual need to do what it takes in the business unless you have an instinctual need to succeed. Many of the successful business owners I know seem to have this instinctual need to succeed. It is drilled so deep inside of them, they will climb any hill, write any program, fix any machine, or wrestle any alligator in order to succeed in their business.

When I explain to people who ask how we were able to grow our business to where it is today, I mention a maniacal commitment to success and the story of Mary Roszel, one of the founders of our first store. I always knew that if, as partners, we decided that it would further the business and help us succeed for Mary to walk from Lansing to Chattanooga, she would go to her closet, get her walking shoes on, and start walking to

Tennessee without asking a question. She was so dedicated to the business, it was awe inspiring. Everybody in the organization knew it, and that commitment level was infectious.

I wish there were a serum we could inject into people who are starting a business that would make them drunk with commitment, allow them to thrive on chaos, and give them boundless energy to wake up every day and bring their A+ game. **There isn't.** I wish there were a playbook that gave you guidelines and rules on what to do in the first twelve to eighteen months of your business. **There isn't.** I wish there were a network of people out there to support people who are living through a start-up. **There isn't.**

Most of the stuff written on "entrepreneurialism" that is meant to support leaders during start-up leads people down the wrong brain path. Most of that stuff focuses on the science of start-up. It walks you through how to write a business plan, what to include in your legal documents (don't forget about your exit strategy in the event the business fails), how an effective marketing plan should be assembled, and—my personal favorite—how to organize your deck to present to investors and raise money.

This is the science, the recipe. This is the nuts and bolts. This is the stuff people focus on when first launching their idea. Doing a wonderful job on these documents represents the likelihood of success about as much as how the owner's manual, a map, and what type of gas you put in your car will determine how successful you will become as a new driver.

The only thing that matters, the only metric I want you thinking about before you start your business, is your commitment

ACKNOWLEDGMENTS

FIRST AND FOREMOST, I must acknowledge and thank my parents, Jim and JoAnn McFall, for constructing such a sturdy platform for me to build upon. Looking back, I am amazed at how carefully and deliberately you designed and assembled my foundation. I am eternally grateful.

Second, my wife Elizaveta is my inspiration to keep growing and pushing myself. You are challenging me to be better every day. You are my beacon, and I know you will guide me to a better, stronger, more meaningful place. All my love.

Third, to my children, Lee, Klava, and Oscar, I am fueled by you and the amazing opportunity you have in front of you. If we all could acknowledge the vast opportunity in front of us, the world would be infinitely more interesting. I can't wait to support you on your journey and see what amazing things you end up seeing and doing.

Fourth, to my brothers, Pat and Curt, a consistent positive force in my life, listening, encouraging, and generally trying to keep me inbounds. Fifth, to the Bombers (Double Deuce, a.k.a. Bob Olson; Tricky, a.k.a. Rick Slaght; Young Bobby, a.k.a. Bobby Dunlap; Danny G., a.k.a. Danny Gagnon; Captain, a.k.a. Aaron Ostrander; Robby; Timmy; JY; Chuck; Matt; Tommy; Woody; Tony D.; Balaka; KC; Romo; TP; Brad the goalie; the Surgeon; Clooner; and more), thank you for being the best friends anybody could ask for.

Finally, to my business partner, Bob Fish, thank you for putting up with my special brand of crazy. The ride has been long and intense, but what always has me excited is the feeling we are just getting started. Thank you for being the greatest partner anybody could ask for.

For everyone I didn't acknowledge that I should have, I made a deliberate decision to keep this to my tightest ring, my closest circle. If I were to go out one more increment, this acknowledgment would be twenty pages long. There are many people to thank in my life, people who have taught me, shared with me, and made me who I am today. I wish I could write a paragraph on each of you, but instead I will just list your name and send you a private note explaining why you are listed here in my first book. My Grandpa Poppenger, Bob Fautek, Bob Washer, Mrs. Heffelbower, John and Judy Kleeves, Cleve King, Jon and Marilynn Steiner, Mr. Marinucci, George Campbell, Mike Soenen, Lewis Miller, Joseph Bangura, Joe Opalla, Johnny Smythe, Uncle Kevin, Jason Woodrum, Heather Sinclair, Mary Roszel, Mohamed Shetiah, Mike Williams, Deb Kirchen, Brooke McFall, Barry Greenblatt, Jan Cunningham, Joe Linstroth, Elena Efimova, and the YPO Ferrari Forum.

For those at work, those who have grown with me for a decade or longer—Tony D., Jeremy, Steph, Laura, Brie—thank you for everything you have taught me. For those just signing on, welcome to our team, and I look forward to the ride with all of you.

A very special thank you to you all.

INTRODUCING THE COWBOY SQUIRREL

THE LEGEND OF THE SQUIRREL: They don't even try to remember where they hide their nuts, and they hide enough so that when they start looking, there are so many around that they are bound to find enough to sustain themselves.

The legend of the cowboy: They don't care what anybody thinks. They are who they are, and tough shit if it doesn't work for you.

Combine the two and you get the Cowboy Squirrel—and you have two of the most important characteristics to be successful in your business.

INDEX

ABOUT THE AUTHOR

MICHAEL J. MCFALL spent his formative years in Highland, Michigan, living on Dunham Lake and graduating from Milford High School in 1989. His junior year, he was a member of the Canadian Class Afloat program, sailing on a square-rigged barkentine tall ship called *Pogoria*. The ship left Louisbourg, Nova Scotia, and sailed to Singapore, stopping in thirteen countries; Mike had dynamic experiences in each of them.

In his senior year, he captained both his hockey and golf teams to two of their best seasons to date. He then attended Kalamazoo College, a small liberal arts school that is a shining star for diversity and inclusion, which solidified Mike's commitment to the causes of equality and opportunity for all. In his junior year of college, he studied in Sierra Leone in West Africa. At the time Mike was studying there, 1991, Sierra Leone was the poorest and least developed country on the planet, according to the World Bank. This experience guided Mike's thoughts, teaching him that no matter where we live, or what circumstances we live within, we are all searching for the same thing: love.

Mike saw a lot of the world at a young age and learned early that similarities in people far outweigh the differences by a factor of one hundred to one. He loves the Arthur Miller quote from *Death of a Salesman*: "We are all searching for the right way to live so we can call the world a home."[2]

Mike graduated and took a job as a straight-commission sales representative in Houston, Texas. He often credits his success in business to the foundation this sales job provided. There are no more valuable lessons in business than waking up and trying to sell a ton of product. If we do that as business-people, we stand a much better chance at being successful. He enjoyed his work in Houston but wanted to be closer to friends and family in Michigan.

Mike moved home and, after a couple of meaningless jobs, landed in Lansing, Michigan, working at a coffee shop called BIGGBY COFFEE as a minimum-wage barista. The owner of the original store, Bob Fish, supported him in getting deeply involved in the business, and they eventually struck up a mutually beneficial partnership to grow and expand the brand and concept of BIGGBY COFFEE. Today Mike is co-CEO with Bob, and BIGGBY has over 250 stores open in 9 states. After

2   Arthur Miller, *Death of a Salesman* (Amereon Ltd., 1949).

twenty-three years, the company is in high growth mode, and the future looks bright.

In the same year that he joined BIGGBY COFFEE, Mike tried out for and made a beer league hockey team that would eventually turn into the BIGGBY Bombers. These guys have been his best friends for twenty-two years. They have quite literally grown up together. Never has there been a better group of guys assembled to play beer-league sports.

Mike lives in Ann Arbor, Michigan, with his wife, Elizaveta, and their three children, Lee, Klava, and Oscar. They are fortunate to have a wonderful community of love that starts with their families and extends to their school community and to their extraordinary friends. Life can be a dream, a fairytale. Mike wakes up every day amazed at how much of his life is exactly how he dreamt it would be.